# glamping getaways

# glamping
# getaways

## stylish stays around the UK

Shelley Bowdler, Sophie Dawson, Keith Didcock, Jonathan Knight,
Andrea Oates, Sam Pow, Amy Sheldrake, Andy Stothert, Clover Stroud,
Alexandra Tilley Loughrey, Richard Waters, Dixe Wills, and Harriet Yeomans
with additional contributions by Paul Marsden, Susan Smith, and Paul Sullivan

# introduction

There's something undeniably special about arriving at your destination to find someone has already made camp for you. No unpacking or lugging, no battling with an unfamiliar tent, no searching for forgotten accessories, or borrowing extra tent pegs. You just arrive, and it's all ready. Fantastic.

Of course, glamping is not a new phenomenon. Centuries ago, explorers blazing trails through the jungles of Asia or the deserts of Africa would send minions ahead to make camp. The VIP explorers would hang back a bit, affecting to survey the wilds and 'discover' things, arriving at camp just as the tents were ready, beds made, and dinner was being served. 'Is that Gin and Tonic for me? Lovely, don't mind if I do. It has been a hard day *discovering*, after all…'

So if we have people like Henry Hudson and George Everest to thank for the concept, we have the good old British newspapers to thank for the term 'glamping', the ingenious fusion of the words 'glamorous' and 'camping'. I guess we should just be grateful that they

didn't opt for pomping (posh camping) or pramping (premium camping).

And so as glamping has made its way into the English language, glampsites, in their various guises, have been popping up all over the UK. Yurts, tipis, gypsy caravans, shepherd's huts, canvas shacks, and chic safari tents now offer a real alternative to a boring B&B or an uninspiring holiday home.

And the innovative people behind such glampsites continue to think outside of the tent. Take Tipi Adventure (p100), for instance, who combine tipi stays with kayaking along the River Wye in Herefordshire. Then there's Livingstone Lodge (p82), which brings a full-size safari adventure to Kent, complete with zebras, rhinos, and giraffes. Or for something less energetic, relax in the woodland sauna at fforest (p164) in Wales, luxuriate in a hot tub outside your gypsy caravan at Mandinam (p136), or enjoy an in-yurt massage at Eco Retreats (p182). This isn't just about the accommodation, it's about the experience – and it's a world away

from the style-by-numbers predictability
of most boutique hotels.

It's worth mentioning, though, that many of
the places in this book are a long way from
the level of luxury you'd expect in a 5-star
hotel. The term 'glamping' is relative; this is
'glamorous for camping', so don't arrive
expecting fawning service, memory-foam
mattresses, and posh toiletries. It's more about
removing the hassles, so you can just turn up,
instantly relax, and enjoy your holiday.

The sites in *Glamping Getaways* are perfect
for regular campers who fancy a bit of luxury,
couples after a cosy break, families in need of
a hassle-free holiday, or first-time campers
wanting to ease their way into a stay under
the stars. The sites invariably involve a magical
setting – hidden away in a secret valley, lost
among the trees of an ancient woodland, or
dotted across a hillside brimming with views.

So, whatever the reason you're off glamping,
you're in for a treat. Pack your own G&T and
take off on your own adventure...

# campsite locator

ISLE OF MULL
Oban `50`
Perth
Dundee
`49`
Glasgow
Dunbar `48`
Edinburgh
Melrose `47`
`30`
Newcastle Upon Tyne
Sunderland
Penrith
Whitby
`29`
`28`
Scarborough
`26`
Morecambe `27`
`25`
Blackpool
Leeds
Kingston Upon Hull
Liverpool
Manchester
Cromer
ISLE OF ANGLESEY `46`
Beaumaris
Sheffield
Betws-y-coed
Stoke -on-Trent
Wells-next-the-Sea
Nottingham
`45`
Lowestoft
`44`
Welshpool
Birmingham
`42`
`43`
Aberystwyth
`40`
`41`
`24`
Cardigan
`38` `39`
Hereford
`23`
`34` `33`
`22`
Cheltenham
St David's
`37`
`32`
Oxford
`36`
`35`
Carmarthen
Monmouth
`21`
`20`
Tenby
`31`
Cardiff
Bristol
London
Margate
Bath
Reading
`19`
Weston-super-Mare
Guildford
Royal Tunbridge Wells
Minehead
`18`
Folkestone
`14`
`16`
`8`
`13`
Brighton
`9`
`15`
Hastings
Poole
`10` `11`
Southampton
`17`
`6`
`7`
Bognor Regis
`12`
Padstow
`3` `4`
Swanage
`1`
`5`
`2`
Plymouth
Torquay
St Ives
Salcombe
Penzance

There's something about heading down an unmarked lane into a Cornish valley that just feels so right. Polgreen's particular unmarked lane slides almost unnoticed into the Vale of Mawgan, a few miles north of Newquay. At the bottom, a sloping field sheltered by woodland and hidden by hedges is host to the satisfyingly retro sight of a scattering of cream-coloured bell tents.

Simon and Sarah, Polgreen's friendly owners, transform this little corner of their 40-acre farm into a glamping haven for just six weeks every summer. Five 5-metre bell tents are positioned on their own little plots of levelled ground with plenty of space around them, while another hides away at the top of the field – tucked around the corner for those who enjoy a bit of privacy or yearn for a sylvan retreat. Each tent is furnished with a double bed, a double futon, a roll-mat bed, a coffee table, a great big rug, and all the pots, pans, crockery, cutlery, and so forth, that usually reside in a kitchen. Further living space is provided by a communal 'chilling' tent, complete with a tarp-roofed dining area, which is a big hit with families.

The facilities, all stationed just the other side of a bridge over a tiny brook, are designed to strike joy into the heart of the eco-conscious camper. Four compost loos are

housed in delightful little sheds replete with antiquated reading matter. The two bijou showers are illuminated inside with solar-powered lights. There's a raised bed from which campers may harvest salad leaves, and pots of herbs with which to garnish the cordon bleu dishes you've whipped up in the BBQ thoughtfully supplied with every pitch.

And there's really no excuse for not cooking up some mouth-watering food here. A 10-minute walk up a track leads to the Gluvian Farm Organics shop, where absolutely everything on sale has been produced on the owners' land (do ask for a taste of their yummy preserves). Barely any distance further away, in the village of Trevarrian, you'll find equally appetising fare at the Bre-Pen Farm Shop. Meanwhile, down in Mawgan Porth, there's a former petrol station – now called Cornish Fresh – that looks like the sort of place that sells seaside holiday tat, but that actually houses a deli with a wide range of ingredients destined to inspire all sorts of culinary greatness.

Polgreen is just a short hop from a clutch of Cornwall's best surfing beaches, as well as some of the most dramatic stretches of the South West Coast Path, so grab your wetsuit or boots and get out there. After a day on the beach, children can help feed Polgreen's horses, pigs, ducks, fish, and two eminently strokeable pet sheep, Rosie and Ruby. The kids can also keep a look out for the array of wildlife on the farm – from otters and roe deer to horseshoe bats, heron, snipe, and even the occasional bittern.

It's a bit of shame that Newquay Airport is just over the hill from Polgreen since it means that when the wind is coming from the wrong direction noise from planes and helicopters can impinge on the tranquillity of the site. However, most of the time all you'll hear is the wind in the trees, the calls of unseen wood pigeons, and, if you listen carefully at night, the hoots and toowits of owls patrolling the dark woods.

## Polgreen Glamping

Polgreen Barn, St Mawgan, Cornwall, TR8 4AG
www.glampingcornwall.com

🐑 There are 6 bell tents (sleeping up to 5) and a communal 'chilling' tent with sofa, board games, mini-bar, and occasional freshly made treats. No campfires are allowed, but each tent has a BBQ.

🐑 Newquay is renowned for its surf schools (Simon and Sarah have surfing equipment they can lend out), but you can also go snorkelling or diving there (01637 850930; www.atlanticdiver.co.uk). The sandy beach at Bedruthan Steps is amazing (though do check tide times first); Padstow and the Camel Trail (see www.sustrans.org.uk) are just 6 miles away; or you can hire a motorboat and chug happily down the river from Fowey Boatyard (01726 832194).

🐑 Take a stroll along a gated lane to manicured St Mawgan, home to the Falcon Inn (01637 860225; www.thefalconinn-stmawgan.co.uk) and its range of local ales. Watergate Bay is the home of Jamie Oliver's Cornish Fifteen (01637 861000; www.fifteencornwall.co.uk) – very pricey but nicey. Right underneath is the less expensive but highly recommended Beach Hut (01637 860877; see www.watergatebay.co.uk). Farm shops worthy of a trip are Gluvian Farm Organics at Mawgan Porth (01637 860635; www.gluvianfarmorganics.co.uk) and Bre-Pen Farm Shop (01637 860420; www.bre-penfarm.co.uk) in Trevarrian.

🐑 The site is open only in July and August.

🐑 Pre-booking is essential. Bell tents £180 per week, plus £18 per person, per night; children (under 13 years) £10 per night; babies in travel cots free.

# tremeer

## Tremeer Yurt Holidays

Tremeer Farm, Lanteglos-by-Fowey, Cornwall, PL23 1NN; www.yurtscornwall.com

The 2 yurts and 1 ger each come surrounded by green space. The funky restored barn has a fully equipped modern kitchen upstairs, including fridge and microwave, and spick and span toilets and hot showers downstairs. There are fire pits for campfires as well as gas and charcoal BBQs outside.

You're right near Polkerris Beach, so get water happy with a bit of sailing, windsurfing, powerboating, and more from the Polkerris Beach Company (01726 813306; www.polkerrisbeach.com). Otherwise grab your hiking boots and explore the South West Coast Path. For a bit of Cornish culture, take a stroll down the narrow winding streets of Fowey old town, and browse the many galleries and shops.

Lots of local produce is available from the farmhouse: there are pork chops, sausages, bacon, and eggs; apple juice and sometimes cider; and milk and bread can be pre-ordered from the milkman. If you fancy a night out then head to nearby Fowey where you'll find Sam's (01726 832273; www.samsfowey.co.uk), an American bistro, which also has a place at Polkerris Beach (01726 812255) with top-notch pasta and the yummiest wood-fired pizzas.

Open from Easter to mid October; in the summer holidays you have to book for full weeks but at other times it's possible to arrange short breaks.

A week costs £350 to £650 (depending on the season).

Hidden away among a warren of high-banked, treelined Cornish lanes, Tremeer Farm offers the ultimate test of your glamping credentials. To the untrained eye, the three structures all look like yurts. But one of these yurts isn't, in fact, a yurt. It's a ger. The distinction between the two comes down to a subtle difference in the curvature of the roof poles, apparently. But the important thing is that they're all cute little pods of canvas cosiness, whatever they happen to be called.

The dwellings are nicely spaced out, giving visitors plenty of room to roam, and all are comfortably furnished with wooden floors, cosy rugs, a wood-burning stove, plus a full-size bed with feather duvet. You can tell that owners Rob and Sarah have lavished lots of love and a good measure of hard work on the transformation of Tremeer from working farm to a beautiful luxury camping destination. But true to the farm's roots, you're bound to bump into one or two animals during your stay. In fact, you may find it hard to avoid pet Kune Kune pigs Rosie and Rollo, who just love a belly rub.

After exploring the hidden coves and stunning walks nearby, soak your tired muscles in the wood-fired cedar hot tub back at camp, before cooking dinner on an open fire – and settling down for a game of 'spot the ger'.

Picture the scene… the atmospheric smell of woodsmoke, the mouth-watering sizzle of a trout caught fresh from a glittering aquamarine lake, and the sound of children's laughter as they play happily outside your tipi. But this isn't a beautiful, directed family scene from the pages of *Vogue*, it's a real and idyllic setting where happy memories are made.

There was a time when camping used to be all about nasty nylon sleeping bags and unpleasantly soggy tents. Then along came the concept of glamorous camping (or, rather, 'glamping'), and suddenly you couldn't move for fashionistas throwing up Alice Temperley-style tipis in the remoter parts of the great British countryside. But what makes Cornish Tipi Holidays a bit different, and, we like to think, a bit special, is that it's the real thing and there isn't a bottle of Coke in sight. Authenticity and longevity are the key words.

Set up in 1997 by Elizabeth Tom and Alan Berry, it was the first commercial tipi campsite in England, and well over a decade down the line it's still going strong. The site's arranged around the stunning spring-fed lake in the old Tregildrans quarry, and it forms a natural eco-system. Breeding hawks soar through the sky, and the tangled edges of the stony paths are a natural haven for moths, butterflies, and even, perhaps, the odd dormouse.

In this wilder-than-wild environment, there's potential for everyone, young and old, to flourish. No surprise, then, to hear that Alice Temperley herself spent her honeymoon here. Now what on earth would Hiawatha have thought about that?

## Cornish Tipi Holidays

Tregeare, Pendoggett, St Kew, Cornwall, PL30 3LW
www.cornishtipiholidays.co.uk

🛶 Forty tipis are scattered around the 16-acre site, with 2 large 'village fields' of 6 and 11 large tipis, interspersed with smaller sites. Every tipi has a lantern, box of utensils, and logs. The site's off the National Grid, so you can really get back to nature. Spend the day by the lake, messing about in a boat or fishing for trout. There's space galore for kids to run around as well as winding paths by sparkling streams and shady woodland to explore.

🛶 Head to Port Isaac (www.portisaac-online.co.uk), a great place for sea-kayaking and buying scallops or crabs. Pick up the Camel Trail near Wadebridge (01460 221162; www.cornishlight.co.uk) and explore the 16 miles John Betjeman described as 'the best journey in England'.

🛶 For groceries use the Spar in Delabole (01840 213897). You can buy excellent pasties from either Auntie Avice (great egg and bacon pie) at St Kew or Cornish Maids in Camelford (01840 212749). The Other Place in Fowey (01726 833636; www.theotherplacefowey.com) does creative fish and chips, including scallops or calamari. The Globe Hotel at Lostwithiel (01208 872501) does excellent Sunday lunches and good midweek sandwiches.

🛶 Open from mid March to early November.

🛶 Cost for a family of 4 in a large tipi ranges from £715 in low season to £860 in high season.

# belle tents

## Belle Tents

Owl's Gate, Davidstow, Camelford, Cornwall, PL32 9XY; www.belletentscamping.co.uk

🏕 The camping field has 3 camps, each with 2 tents: a twin and a double, sleeping 4–6 people. Each tent has cutlery, firewood, a BBQ, and a cooker. At night the site's lit by solar markers, which you can use as nightlights.

🏕 The sandy delights of the north coast are 5 miles away; Tintagel Castle (01840 770328; www.tintagelcastle.co.uk) and beach is great for a day out. Polzeath beach (www.polzeathincornwall.co.uk) is great for surfing, with surf schools jostling for space beside ice-cream shops.

🏕 Foodwise, you can cook on the communal fire (or the undercover BBQ), using produce and herbs growing on site. Shop for organic fruit and veg at Hill Top Farm shop (01840 211518), just 5 minutes away. There's a Co-op, fish-and-chip shop, and Chinese takeaway in Camelford, and the Masons Arms (01840 213309) does great food, especially local sea bass and mussels.

🏕 Open from May to the end of September.

🏕 A twin will set you back £380 per week; a week in a 4–6-person camp costs £550 to £640; or rent the whole site for £1540 to £1740 per week.

Who says that camping has to be about serried ranks of boring beige tents? These stripey beauties look like delicious strawberry Cornettos and make camping here a complete doddle – everything you can think of is already provided. Utter camping bliss!

Poet John Betjeman, synonymous with all things truly 'English', earmarked Cornwall as his favourite place in the entire country and he wrote about it a great deal. He's buried at the church at St Enodoc, for all those campers who wish to pay him homage. So, because Cornwall is truly Betjeman-country, it's completely appropriate that you can camp in a bell tent, reading to your children from *A Ring of Bells* or to yourself from the grown-up version *Summoned by Bells*, while in the distance you can make out the sound of the bells of St Endellion church. It really is a beautifully beguiling thing.

Belle Tents is a fantastic place for wildlife spotting, so any budding naturalist can have a field day, particularly in the evenings, when butterflies and moths flit around the wild garden as the sun starts to dip in the sky.

But however you choose to fill your time during your stay, there's something magically theatrical about being here. The tents are set up like a medieval encampment, reminding all of us of times gone by.

Hippies at heart, site owners Laura and Dave make these wonderful tents themselves. Their studio is just beside this sunny, south-westerly-facing site, which is also home to rare-breed cattle and ponies grazing in nearby fields. Such a stunning setting might just inspire you to write some poetry of your own.

yurtcamp

Like to holiday with your kids but need some 'me' time, too? Then step this way. At this tipi-tastic haven you can let the kids run wild in the woods every morning while you wake up in a leisurely fashion over a freshly poured, frothy cappuccino in the café. Then, when you're ready, slowly wander back to your camp and dig out a good book. You could be on your own for a while.

The best thing about yurt camping is you don't have to fiddle about with tents. And the best thing about Yurtcamp is that you don't need to plan many days out. Within this 40-acre fern paradise are two assault courses with tyre swings, nets, and rope bridges, plus various winding trails to follow, and a partly covered playroom with giant-sized games.

Yurtcamp sits on the edge of Dartmoor, the largest expanse of moorland in the south of England, and a Site of Special Scientific Interest. A stay here does come with a hum of motorway traffic in the background depending on where you are (you can't hear it in the woods), but the sound becomes as insignificant as that of a buzzing bee once you get used to it.

Nine yurts are dotted in a circle in The Village, an area that can be block-booked by groups (Totnes, Torquay, and Exeter are nearby for a big night out). You have to bring your own towels but there are trolleys in the car park that make lugging your stuff to your yurt less of a chore. Each yurt contains up to four beds, a cooker, table, cool box, and chairs. The café sells breakfasts (the vegetarian option is popular after a few BBQs), and West Country cider and local beers in the early evening.

## Yurtcamp

Gorse Blossom Farm, Staplehill Road, Liverton, Devon, TQ12 6JD; www.yurtcamp.co.uk

🏕 Nineteen yurts (with 6, 4, or 2 beds) sleeping 100 people in total on site. They're hand-made, which is great, and quite rustic; some rugs on the wooden floor would be most welcome. The Village has 9 yurts, the rest are scattered around the woodland. The shower block is super-clean and modern with 9 showers and 12 loos. The café-bar opens mornings and evenings, selling proper coffee, breakfasts, meals, and snacks including Devonshire ice creams. Family games include a high zip-wire, giant Connect 4, table tennis, pool, and skittles. Free ice packs, and freezer access; an 'honesty' washing machine, cooking fire pits with grills (remember to bring charcoal). Sadly, campfires are not allowed.

🏕 Whatever the weather, jump in and make a splash at Becky Falls waterfalls (01647 221259; www.beckyfalls.com). There's so much more to discover there besides the eponymous cascade – animal-related fun at the zoo as well as a range of walks, from challenging to easy, around the park.

🏕 Hike for 2 hours or drive for 20 minutes to Rock Inn (01364 661305; www.rock-inn.co.uk) in Dartmoor National Park. The former 1700s coaching inn has a splendid view of Haytor Rocks and more puddings (Bakewells, brownies, brûlées… you name it) than are healthy for just one visit.

🏕 Open from March to late December.

🏕 The cost varies: £225 to £795, depending on the size of yurt, time of year, and length of stay.

# summerhill farm

Passion. It either burns within you, or it doesn't. Enthusiasm can be faked, but a true passion for something can't. And Ben has passion: for the animals on the farm he rents from the Soil Association, for organic agriculture, and for sharing his beautiful surroundings with those in need of a well-earned escape to the countryside.

When his wife Alice has work, Ben tends the 90-acre organic farm alone; lovingly rearing his 500 hens, 200 geese, flock of sheep, and herd of pure-bred Red Ruby cows. So, when folk come to stay in one of the three yurts or two bell tents on the farm, he's only too happy to stop for a chat and ask if they're enjoying their stay. The answer is always a resounding 'Yes!'.

Not only are the views down the valley from each tent stunning, but every possible care has gone into furnishing them too. Each comes stocked with tea, coffee, sugar, milk, bread, butter, and eggs (courtesy of Ben's hens) to make settling in a breeze after the journey down to Devon. Charcoal and kindling are also provided free of charge for the fire pits, stove, and chimenea; as are candles, a torch, bedding, and towels. In fact, you won't need to pack much at all.

You don't even need to go food shopping; it's all here – in the converted barn next to the comfy campers' lounge, with wood-burning stove, games, pool table, and info, is a huge kitchen with an 'honesty' fridge and larder. All the food on offer has a price sticker and you just leave the cash in a box. And if you're lucky there'll be a bowl of delicious, free home-grown veg that needs eating up. Each dwelling has its own large fridge in the kitchen so you can fill it with goodies to your heart's content. Or even pre-order one of the Hampers for Campers on offer here, stocked with as much produce as the farm can provide, and other food and drink produced from the local area.

Each of the three yurts sits atop insulating wooden decking and looks down the valley and across to the hills opposite. Two are large

Mongolian yurts that sleep up to six and the other is a smaller structure sleeping four or five. The bell tents have their own private corner in a separate field with vistas out to Exmoor, behind. They're smaller than the yurts and have fewer furnishings, but still come with a bed and futon mattresses for comfort.

Campers are welcome to help out on the farm if they wish – collecting eggs from the hens or picking veg from the polytunnel and colourful beds. As this is Soil Association land, various eco-friendly measures are implemented as a salute to the beautiful surrounding scenery. Not only is the farming here of the sustainable variety, facilities are provided courtesy of Mother Nature herself. Summerhill's hot water is produced through solar panels on the barn's roof, and electricity is generated through a photovoltaic system (more panels), which cuts $CO_2$ emissions and often provides surplus electricity that's fed back into the National Grid. Impressive stuff.

For a means of diversification for an organic farmer and a start-up site, Summerhill Farm strikes the perfect balance between working farm, campsite, environmental caretaker, and lovely holiday. And as some of Ben's passion will most definitely have rubbed off on you by the time you leave, you'll be sure to be booking a return visit as soon as you're home.

## Summerhill Farm

Summerhill Farm, Hittisleigh, Exeter, Devon, EX6 6LP
www.summerhill-farm.co.uk

Every care and thought for guests has been put into each of the 3 yurts and 2 bell tents. They come with everything but the kitchen sink. Campfires are allowed in fire pits (each abode has one, as well as a BBQ and picnic table). Plans are afoot to erect another yurt further down the valley, with its own eco-shower and compost loo to keep it self-contained – so watch this space. If you're staying in the bell tents, which are furthest from the farm, it's a bit of a trek to the facilities. Marked walks take you around the farm's many acres, including down to the river at the valley floor for a splash or stone skim. Maps of the farm's boundaries are available from the communal barn.

The vast and sandy beach at Bude (check the tide times) is a 40-minute drive away; or closer to home there's the riverside walk at Fingle Bridge; and for a spot of history head to Castle Drogo (01647 433306; see www.nationaltrust.org.uk) in Drewsteignton.

You're on an organic farm so take advantage of the delicious home-grown produce and that of the local area by pre-ordering one of the Hampers for Campers. The 'honesty' larder and fridge in the kitchen is stocked with organic fruit bags and veg boxes, meat, eggs, and local juices and ciders. If you want to eat out, the Mulberry (01647 24227; www.themulberrydevon.com) lies 4 miles away in Cheriton Bishop and serves excellent if pricey meals.

Open from early April to the end of September.

Stays cost between £200 and £475. Weekend, midweek break, and full week prices vary according to season and which dwelling you opt for.

cuckoo down
farm

Decadence is, of course, meant to be a bad thing. It did for the bright young things of the thirties, and is even said to have caused the downfall of the mighty Roman Empire. But, when you're receiving a fantastic massage in a yurt at a quiet Devon hideaway, it's difficult not to wonder whether those youthful aristocrats and the Caesars had the right idea after all.

Several hundred metres down a track off the edge of the village of West Hill, the 30-acre Cuckoo Down Farm is home to a scattering of black-faced sheep, some horses, a pony, a clucktch of chickens, and, at the top of a large open field, three yurts. Each one is furnished with a lovely double bed as well as two convertible sofas, a coffee table, a very efficient wood-burning stove, and various other bits and bobs including a vase of freshly cut flowers. On the floor, large rugs spread themselves languorously across the carpet.

Wander outside and you'll find not only your own compost loo, but your own kitchen too – a wooden shelter containing all the culinary perquisites you'll need to knock up something special to serve at your picnic table. Showers are a short stroll away in a barn by the farmhouse. Meanwhile, fresh innovations include a communal circus-like tent, a gypsy caravan, a 'retro' caravan, and (in a separate field) a couple of safari tents.

And in addition to booking a visit from Penny and her magical massage fingers, you can also call on the in-yurt services of a reflexologist, a yoga teacher, a reiki healer, and even an art therapist – all, happily, at extremely undecadent prices.

## Cuckoo Down Farm Yurts

Lower Broad Oak Road, West Hill, Ottery St Mary, Devon, EX11 1UE; www.luxurydevonyurts.co.uk

🌿🦆 There's a fire pit, kitchen, and compost loo by each of the 3 yurts. Three nice big showers are located in a barn near the farmhouse (along with a fridge-freezer, washing machine, and tumble-dryer). Kids can play in Cuckoo Down stream, make dens in woods, collect eggs from chickens (there's an 'honesty' box), and pet and brush the pony.

🌿🦆 Sidmouth (www.visitsidmouth.co.uk), the self-styled seaside heaven, is one of England's classic old-school coastal resorts. The Jurassic Coast (www.jurassiccoast.com), meanwhile, stretches from Exmouth all the way to Swanage in Dorset and offers all manner of fossil-hunting expeditions.

🌿🦆 By the river in Tipton St John, the Golden Lion Inn (01404 812881; www.goldenliontipton.co.uk) sports an outdoor bar and French–English cuisine using local produce. Sidmouth's Dairy Shop deli and café (01395 513018) is packed to the rafters with delicious regional foods.

🌿🦆 Open from early April to the end of September.

🌿🦆 A yurt (sleeps 4 adults or a family of 6) costs £465 to £585 per week (depending on the season). Midweek and weekend breaks are available too.

Wanting a romantic weekend break with a cosy twist? Needing to escape the trappings of modern life? Well swing on over to Somerset, because it's all here. And it's all yours.

The pull at this place is the pretty, colourful, bow-top gypsy caravan, as there are hardly any available for hire in England. And it delivers: on romance, on sentimentality, and on cosiness. You'll find it tucked away in a picture-perfect apple orchard on the edge of the owner's smallholding, so it'll be surrounded by apples or blossom, depending on the season you visit in; and year round you'll be able to enjoy the menagerie – donkeys, dogs, and ducks. It's delightful.

Inside the painted bow-top is a ready-made wooden bed – or 'cot' – that you clamber up into, which would have been folded away for transit in times past. And there's not much room for anything else – this is inside-out living. The original heavy-bottomed pots are stored in a hatch at the back, below your 'bedroom' window. And outside is a fire pit, so you can sit on the wooden steps and watch your kettle boil or sausages sizzle.

And then there's the surprise. You arrive at the orchard expecting to spy just the gypsy caravan and are presented with two other camping-related structures. Don't worry, your romantic weekend won't be spoilt by anyone

else, these are all for you and you alone. Owner Martyn has renovated a charming shepherd's hut that houses your solar-powered power shower and washbasin. This is an eco set-up, where all waste water flows into the ground to nourish willow saplings. There's also an immaculate compost loo.

And in a nod towards kitsch camping – in all its gleaming white and chrome glory – is a 1970s Marshall caravan. This is a visual affront initially, but, frankly, a necessity if the weather's really grim. It also houses a fridge, cooker, and lots of space for you to stretch out in during the day if the bow-top gets a little too snug. In true traveller-style the gypsy caravan is furnished with brass ornaments. Not to everyone's taste, you might think, but our guess is that by the end of your stay you'll be secretly sad to shut the door on it all.

## Gypsy Caravan Breaks

Marsh Farm, Pitney, Langport, Somerset, TA10 9AN
www.gypsycaravanbreaks.co.uk

🌿 Just 1 cosy caravan for 2: you and the one you love will be the only people enjoying this unique camping experience. As well as being able to snuggle up in an original bow-top gyspy caravan, you're also spoilt for choice with the complementary options put on by the thoughtful owner. The downside is that you probably won't want to leave.

🌿 You're surrounded by the Somerset Levels, edged by the Quantock and Mendip Hills, and there are lovely walks just metres from your front door. Glastonbury is within a 15-minute drive, with its cool vibe and famous Tor (www.glastonbury.co.uk). Wells (www.wellstourism.com) offers beautiful architecture, including its famous cathedral, and hosts a twice-weekly farmers' market.

🌿 This is cider country, so be sure to visit one of the many local farms that will happily welcome you for a tasting – or three. The onsite visitors' book gives recommendations. The local pub, the Halfway House (01458 252513), just down the road at Pitney, serves excellent home-cooked meals. You'll find a little starter pack of local produce (and cider) in the fridge in the Marshall caravan when you arrive, and if you fancy some home cooking (campfires are allowed) then head to the Pitney Farm Shop (01458 253002; www.pitneyfarmshop. co.uk) to stock up on local produce. Chances are you won't want to stray much further afield, anyway, with all that tranquillity in your own private orchard.

🌿 Open from April to October.

🌿 From £75 per night; the nightly price gets cheaper the more nights you book.

# stock gaylard

## Stock Gaylard

Sturminster Newton, Dorset, DT10 2BG; www.stockgaylard.com

🌿 There are 2 camps with 3 yurts each (and a spare bell tent). You can build a campfire in a designated fire pit.

🌿 Wear the kids out at Coolplay (01258 474666; www.coolplay.biz) in Sturminster Newton; it has rope bridges, ball pools, tubes, and much more. Older kids will know that Glastonbury festival (www.glastonburyfestivals. co.uk) takes place on the other side of the A303 at Pilton, so revellers should book a night or two here for post-festival R&R. The Oak Fair in the wood every August Bank Holiday Saturday is a more subdued but popular affair.

🌿 Come in early September to experience Sturminster Newton's Cheese Festival (www.cheesefestival.co.uk). Take a right turn out of the estate to find the award-winning Dorset Blue Soup (01963 23133; www.dorsetblue.com) at Woodbridge Farm. The estate also sells veg boxes (£25), eggs (£2 for 12), and even a venison box (about £110).

🌿 Open from May to mid September.

🌿 Weekly yurt rental is £425 to £575; a mini-break is £283 to £380; an entire camp costs £675 to £975 a week (depending on the season).

Oh to live on a country estate. To throw open one's windows and breathe in dawn's mist before it fades away in time for morning birdsong. To see herds of deer frolicking among ancient woodland… The Stock Gaylard pile might itself be out of bounds to everyone bar the resident landed gentry, but, not ones to rest on their laurels, the family owners have created not one but two 'luxury' wonderments on the estate for the hoi polloi.

Two separate yurt camps (Withybed and Brickles) are set in private, secluded clearings of old oaks and elms, alongside nesting owls, nightingales, and butterflies. Withybed, next to the deer park, faces the setting sun, while Brickles has far-reaching views towards Bulbarrow Hill in the east. In both camps three home-made lattice-framed yurts, topped with green camouflaging roofs, perch on wooden platforms. Two yurts are for sleeping in, with a double bed and two single beds crafted to curve with the walls. The interior furnishings both look and feel extravagant.

Outside, the attention to detail continues with fire pits, picnic benches with log seats, a sink, and a tin bath. There's even an empty bell tent for extra guests who bring their own bedding, so in total each camp can sleep 15. The third yurt in each camp serves as a living space and is roomy, with a long sofa,

guidebooks, and wooden dressers containing every kitchen utensil imaginable, except perhaps an Aga, which really wouldn't look out of place at all in this 5-star country camp.

# mudeford
# beach huts

## Mudeford Beach Huts

The Spit, Mudeford, Dorset, BH23 9ND; www.beach-huts.com/mudeford

🏖 A year's worth of huts – 365 in total – are crammed on to the sand spit in various colours and states of decor. Each sleeps 4 people on average and most have a little galley kitchen, with some sort of cooker – and some even have a TV. Other facilities vary according to hut. Water is available from standpipes along the spit and there are 5 loo and shower blocks. You have to bring your own bedding. Pets are not permitted.

🏖 There are several beaches within a drive or boat-ride. Highcliffe is popular with boogie-boarders, and you can reach sandy Southbourne on an open-top bus. Take a fishing trip (07979 081934) from nearby Poole. You can even head across to the Isle of Wight for the day on the Wightlink (www.wightlink.co.uk) from Lymington.

🏖 The laid-back Beach House Café (01202 423474) is the hub of the community. Hang out on the sheltered terrace overlooking the marina and enjoy a huge variety of modern British grub. It also offers an amazingly well-stocked kiosk selling anything that you might have forgotten. Fish fanatics will appreciate the stall on the quay, where you can buy locally caught turbot and skate in season, or some fresh snacks to nibble on there and then.

🏖 Open from early March to the end of October. It can feel cramped and frenetic during high season so, if you can, opt for a more peaceful off-season stay.

🏖 Up to £450 per week for 4 people.

Forming one of the arms of Christchurch's hugging harbour, Mudeford's sand spit offers award-winning beaches and beach huts galore: one for every day of the year, in fact. Some may compare it to a shed shanty town as so many huts are crammed into quite a small space, but no one can bash the fabulous location.

Some huts are extremely chic, while others are decidedly shabby, but the variety of colours is simply fabulous. Originally intended to be sweet little places to change into your swimsuit or make a cup of tea of an afternoon, they're now more often than not stuffed full of overnighters. A peaceful haven this is not, but it's a loveable one all the same.

The huts either overlook the Isle of Wight or Mudeford Harbour, so you're ideally placed for some great sunsets and rises. Even if it's raining you can snuggle up inside the hut and peer out through the condensation. It's a great place to watch the world go by: the Needles are across the bay and there are always fishing nets and lobster pots being unloaded on the quay.

Not all the huts are available for hire and the facilities they offer vary enormously. They sleep four on average and some have a tiny mezzanine floor; perfect for squeezing in a couple of kids. Some run on solar power, some on gas, and some have no electricity at all. Most have a little galley kitchen, with some sort of cooker. So, do your research before plumping for a particular one.

There's a touch of Toytown about the place and, while it's not everyone's cone of winkles, for novelty factor it scores an easy 10 out of 10.

really green
holiday
company

*Cool Camping*'s team of not-so-intrepid campistadors arrived at the Really Green Holiday Company's base camp on the Isle of Wight, with that old classic 'Suspicious Minds' droning along strongly in the back of their cranial containers and wondering just how green a holiday company can really be.

It was mid May when they entered the private world of Afton Park, near Freshwater; the summer was just beginning to cast its glorious green spell across the English countryside, and that cynicism went straight out of the window with the first incredulous glimpse of a dreamy – almost spectral looking – yurt village that seemed to float in a swirl of arboreal blossom. They were half expecting a maiden dressed in flowing white lace to mysteriously appear, gliding through the flowers in a perfect TV advert (for hair products or anti-ageing potions), and their hearts melted completely.

The setting of the Really Green Holiday Company is so gorgeous that the presumed environmental reference in the name now seemed irrelevant in some ways. But the important question, after settling down after this sensual overload, is how green is the Really Green Holiday Company? Can any holiday that retains a measure of comfort and convenience be environmentally harmless?

The green credentials here start before you even get near the place, with visitors being encouraged to leave their cars at home. The Really Green Holiday Company will pick you up from the ferry (which links with the railway network) and arrange cycle hire, bus 'rover' tickets, or even fix you up with a complete walking holiday package.

'Yurters' can get fresh, local, organic food (in natural and minimal packaging) delivered prior to their arrival – and throughout their stay. There's even an organic café and shop within the orchard, if cooking the greens yourself isn't on the holiday menu.

The onsite eco-measures start with the yurts, which are made in time-honoured fashion and from traditional materials. There is no electricity on site, and it is possible to cook outside on open fires, though the mess tent does have gas appliances should the open fire be one eco-step too far. The two compost loos are contrasting in their set-ups; one a hi-tech Swedish contraption, the other – the toilet in the sky – sits above a manually rotated recycled oil drum. Liquid waste is processed naturally through the adjacent reed beds. The shower is a cunning solar-heated device with a log-burner back-up, and it should really be starting to dawn by now that the really remarkable thing is that while this certainly is a really green holiday option, it is a really comfortable and beautiful one too.

So, to get back to the question: can any holiday this comfortable and appealing be truly eco-friendly? Perhaps not totally, but the Really Green Holiday Company is probably as good as it gets.

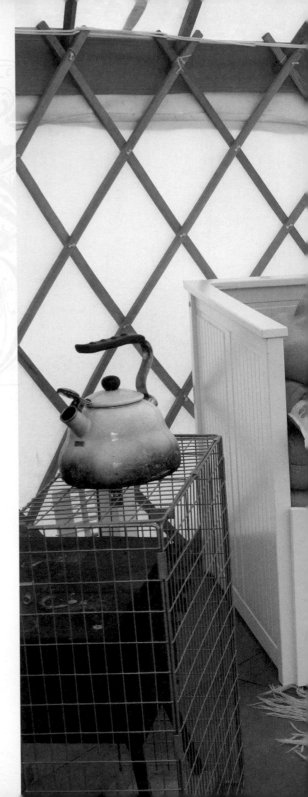

## Really Green Holiday Company

The Apple Farm at Afton Park, Newport Road,
Freshwater Bay, Isle of Wight, PO40 9XR
www.thereallygreenholidaycompany.com

🐑 The 5 yurts (each sleeping 5) are really quite luxurious and equipped with recycled but decent furniture and a wood-burning stove for those chilly late- and early-season evenings. Most folk opt to cook outside on each yurt's log-burning brazier/BBQ.

🐑 The Isle of Wight is packed with options for everyone, with the nearest being the beautiful beach and seaside scenes at Freshwater Bay, just a 10-minute stroll down the road. The cliff walk from Freshwater Bay to the Needles (about 3 miles) is quite remarkable. Another really appealing eco-friendly holiday idea is a visit to Goodleaf Tree Climbing (www.goodleaf.co.uk), on the other side of the island – eminently pedal-able if you're fit, or easily accessed on the excellent local buses (www.islandbuses.info), which also come in handy for some great one-way walking expeditions. The island also has a very good cycle-path network.

🐑 Besides the onsite organic shop and café, Kings Manor Farm Shop and Café in Freshwater (01983 754401; www.kingsmanorfarm.co.uk) has good organically produced meat. The Red Lion (01983 754925) in Freshwater was voted 'best pub on the Isle of Wight' in 2010, and boasts flagstone floors, real ales, and good food. Wash it all down with a visit to Rossiters Vineyard (01983 761616) to sample the local plonk and partake in a guided tour.

🐑 Open from April to October.

🐑 A week's yurt rental is £345 to £595; weekend £220 to £295, and midweek breaks £175 to £295 (depending on the season).

# vintage
# vacations

Not all things American are our cup of tea, but we have to admit that the slick, stylish Airstream trailer is a joy to behold. And those Yanks certainly know how to do luxury camping – they've been doing it since the 1930s. So, what great luck that we, too, can experience an all-American Airstream 'caravan' on the quintessentially English Isle of Wight.

After a short ferry trip from the mainland you'll arrive at Vintage Vacations' field just outside Ryde. The field itself is a pretty ordinary affair with plenty of peace and quiet, hedges and trees around the edges, and that grassy stuff in the middle. But this field is also one of the most extraordinary in England, because gathered around the perimeter, like a wagon-train camp from an old Hollywood western, are 11 of the most remarkable Airstream and Spartan trailers in existence. So remarkable, in fact, that a visit to see this caravan collection is on the curriculum of a degree course in 20th-century culture.

The word 'caravan' hardly seems sufficient for these magnificent articles of metallic sculpture, but when you look inside the sleek, silver, aircraft-like exteriors, that's what they are. So, how did they get here? And why? Well, as it turns out, it's the result of a moment or two of madness, mixed with a dash of impetuosity, and then a whole heap of dedication.

Frazer Cunningham and Helen Carey are the instigators of this amazing field-full of awe-inspiring aluminium, and it all started with a spark of spontaneous purchasing on eBay in 2003, when Frazer and Helen (who is

especially caught up in the style and nostalgia
of these silver specimens) found themselves
the proud, but baffled owners of a wonderful-
looking iconic 1965 Airstream Tradewind
– the kind we've all seen in the movies.

But what were they going to do with
this trailer now it was theirs and looking so
gleamingly inviting? They decided to dip their
toes into the holiday-hire business, and when
the demand for an Airstream 'vacation'
expanded it was time to acquire more of them
from across the pond; restore them to their
original glory; and throw in some of the
stylish retro touches that Helen revels in.

They have 11 in total now, and each one
has been kitted out with an interior and
accessories to recreate mini-worlds of homage
to that innocent golden era of the 50s and 60s.
The exteriors of these silver dream machines
are all irresistibly impressive, and eye-catching
too, but it is the attention to detail inside that
constantly jolts the senses and lifts the spirits.

Holidaying at Vintage Vacations isn't so
much hiring a caravan, or even just hiring a
very special caravan, it's more akin to being
transported to another less-complicated time:
when kitsch was king, girls were girls, boys
were boys, and music was music.

Helen has also now taken a fancy to British
caravans from the 60s, so if the American ones

are too obvious and ostentatious for your
restrained English tastes, then some smaller
nostalgic options are now available. And if
you're all for ostentation and wish to arrive
by helicopter, you'll just need to give some
notice so that Frazer has time to get to work
painting a large H in the middle of the field.

Could it get any better? Well, perhaps, if
they threw in a 1963 Ford Thunderbird
convertible that would be nice, just to ensure
that when you reluctantly leave the Airstream
to explore the island, you could take some of
this retro-chic rock 'n' roll drama with you.

## Vintage Vacations

Hazelgrove Farm, Ashey Road, Ryde, Isle of Wight, PO33 4BD; www.vintagevacations.co.uk

🏕 All the caravans (some sleep 2, 4, and one can fit a family of 6) have a fully equipped kitchen. All have a radio, CD player, and hairdryer, plus all manner of bits and pieces from the 50s and 60s. Each caravan has a shower, but toilets are available only in the site's ablutions block where there are further showers and washing-up facilities. The American caravans have wood-burners, but campfires are not allowed. They don't allow dogs either.

🏕 The Isle of Wight has plenty to offer, including off-road cycle tracks; a whole series of routes can be downloaded from the Wightlink Ferries website (www.wightlink.co.uk). Blackgang Chine (01983 730330; www.blackgangchine.com) is a perfect place in which to continue the nostalgic theme, with a weird selection of childish attractions that seem to appeal just as much to adults (admission is fairly pricey, though). And for more history perfectly preserved, take a trip around Queen Victoria's residence of Osborne House (01983 200022; see www.english-heritage.org.uk).

🏕 In Ryde, Liberty's Café Bar (01983 811007; www.libertyscafebar.co.uk) is highly recommended for being appropriately stylish for Vintage Vacationers, and the food is excellent, though not the cheapest. Grab another bite of nostalgia at the traditional café in the market hall. The Taverners (01983 840707; www.thetavernersgodshill.co.uk) in Godshill – a scrumptiously cute village – is a quaint old pub, some 12 miles away, serving really good food at reasonable prices.

🏕 Open from April to October.

🏕 Prices range from £145 for a 2-night midweek stay in low season to £625 per week in high season.

# meon springs

## Meon Springs Yurt Village

Coombe Road, West Meon, Hampshire, GU32 1HW; www.meonsprings.com

🐾 The Yurt Village is made up of 5 yurts, each sleeping up to 6 people. The yurts are well spaced and shaded by young trees, but not so separate that you feel like a hermit. Ablutional arrangements are provided in toilet blocks. In the Yurtery you'll find all the facilities you'll need.

🐾 Meon Springs also does fly-fishing lessons within a mile from the yurts. Petersfield Lido (www.petersfieldpool. org) is nearby for hot summer days. Take a picnic lunch up to Old Winchester Hill, where there's a Roman hill fort.

🐾 Stock up on food at the butcher's and local shop, both in nearby East Meon. The café at Meon Springs Fishery Lodge is great for snacks and breakfasts. East Meon's Ye Olde George Inn (www.yeoldegeorgeinn.net) is a 15th-century coaching inn with an organic-heavy menu of tasty fare, such as fish pie and roasted rump of lamb.

🐾 Open late March to early November.

🐾 A week's stay in a yurt costs £495 to £785 (depending on the season).

Hampshire's countryside is far from lacking in the scenic stakes: from the mystical woods of its New Forest in the south to the rolling cornfields of its northerly borders, you'll find endless valleys and wild meadows without a person in sight, save the occasional farmer harvesting the crops.

It's in this landscape that you'll find West Meon, a delightfully twee English village that would make an excellent cameo in a *Miss Marple* story. It's also home to Meon Springs Yurt Village. Based on a dairy and arable farm that has been run by the Butler family for three generations, it is one of the few farms in the area that still has dairy cows.

The Yurt Village is run by Jamie and Alison, who conceived the idea in 2009. Other sites may also have yurts from Mongolia, but this campsite actually feels Mongolian. With its miles of china-blue sky and rolling uninterrupted land, this is a place to free the mind and strip away stress.

Inside, the yurts are delightfully rustic, with wood-burning stoves (logs provided), chequer-quilted double beds, and exquisitely hand-painted blue supporting posts, backdropped by wooden cross-hatched fretwork. The accommodation sleeps up to six, and all your bedding and utensils are provided. Outside, you have your own fire pit and a BBQ for cooking under the stars; and on a clear night this is a great spot to gaze skywards to spy a shooting star or ruminate on UFOs.

Come the morning there's loads to do, be it catching trout with a spot of fly fishing, taking a look around the dairy farm, or sampling local ales in pubs as old as Dick Turpin. And while you're out walking or cycling the miles of local paths (Jamie or Alison will give you a map of walks on arrival), you can see who'll be first to bag a lesser-spotted human being.

manor farm

On the edge of the stunning South Downs Park, hidden behind hawthorn hedges and a fortress of burnished wheat fields, is Manor Farm. Blink and you might drive past the tumbledown church next to a working, busy farm. On closer inspection, this idyllic farm campsite is anything but normal. For a start there's a llama called Alfie peering at you from behind his thick woolly coat, and scattered around a lush, green meadow are the most gorgeously welcoming tents we've come across in the whole of Sussex and Hampshire.

The safari tents are a bit like the Tardis – average-sized on the outside, but brilliantly spacious inside. With their wooden floors, Swiss chalet-style bedrooms, wood-burners, ornate lamps, coffee grinders, rustic kitchen tables, and candelabras, we'd like to live here all the time, not just come for a brief holiday.

Run by Anna and her husband Will, Manor Farm's campsite is, in fact, part of the Feather Down Farms family, a group of sites sharing a similar ethos on sustainability and a deep appreciation of the environment. Wander past free-range chickens and pigs to the Pantry Shop for a bowl of locally made ice cream, and pick up some of the farm's bacon for breakfast. Keep an eye out, too, for Anna's home-made Bolognese sauce or farmhouse beef stew, both of which can be purchased.

What you do here is up to you; sit on your stoop like Huckleberry Finn, pondering the candyfloss clouds over the maize fields, or wander down to Selborne village to stock up on provisions. Kids play cricket and footie, you build your fire, your BlackBerry sits in your bag unattended, and your pulse begins to slow to that of a free-diver's. Camping was never supposed to be this easy.

## Manor Farm

West Worldham, Alton, Hampshire, GU34 3BD
www.featherdownfarm.co.uk

There are 7 safari-style tents. The Pantry sells basic food supplies plus pre-cooked dishes. Tents have a flushing loo but the shower block is separate. A BBQ barrel and breakfast hamper is given to you on arrival (plus an unlimited supply of logs for the wood-burner). Campfires are allowed in individual, private fire pits, which are provided. There are 650 acres to explore (perhaps on one of the farm's buggy tours), plus a menagerie of animals. Kids can hunt for fresh eggs in the chicken coop and watch lambs being born in spring. Cycle hire with child seats available (adult/child £8.50/£5.50 per day).

Head to nearby Portsmouth Dockyard – rich in history and jaw-droppingly ferocious warships – or the magical New Forest (www.thenewforest.co.uk). Closer still is Alice Holt Forest (www.aliceholt.org), home of Go Ape (08456 439215; www.goape.co.uk). Zip wires stretch across the trees inviting you to throw yourself into the woody abyss suspended by a cable. Forest bike hire is available from Quench Cycles (01420 520355; www.quenchcycles.co.uk).

You can order bread and pastries to be delivered in the morning, and gather round in the evening to cook pizzas in the alfresco bread oven. If the Pantry doesn't satisfy you, head over to the cosy Selborne Arms (01420 511247; www.selbornearms.co.uk). The bar features local ales and an earthy menu, with dishes such as Welsh rarebit and bubble and squeak.

Open early April to the end of October.

Each safari tent sleeps up to 6. Weekly rental is £435 to £845; weekends cost £295 to £589.

billycan
camping

If you're born in Arundel you're known as a mullet – not because it's a given that you'll have a laughable hairdo, but due to the presence of mullet in the River Arun, which cuts quietly through this West Sussex town and bestows it with even more charm than surely it has a right to. In fact, were you an Anglophile, you might just fall over in a paroxysm of awe as you take in its cobbled side streets, quaintly wilting facades of timber and brick houses, and the twin 'bookends' of its cathedral and its imposing castle, sitting on opposing hills pondering one another.

There are bric-a-brac shops aplenty, antiques boutiques, old-world cafés, and a clutch of first-class restaurants to keep any foodie blissfully quiet. Arundel rises from flat meadows up a modest hillside and was given fair-trade status a few years ago; you'll see there's a real force here towards organic, locally produced food.

You'd do well to start your visit at the castle itself; built in the late 11th century under the reign of William the Conqueror, it's been in the family of the Duke of Norfolk for over 800 years and its handsome, fairy-tale looks have seen it used in TV series as varied as *Doctor Who* (tell that one to the kids) and *MacGyver*, and the Oscar-winning film *The Madness of King George*.

Equally regal for its stunning views of the castle town and the majesty of its natural environment in wild meadows, is Billycan Camping. If you're looking for style and comfort combined with an earthiness that takes you back to the days of your camping forays as a child, then you're in luck. In the words of its co-founder Alex: 'We're family camping, not glamping... a place where kids can meet and like-minded adults get together around the communal campfire.' But don't let

her fool you entirely, for while the bell tents, tipis, and their setting may be rustic, the style of the place is really something else. How many campsites have a communal safari tent that looks like a Bedouin palace – with fur throws on the floor, Moroccan lamps, and wicker chairs? This place is beautifully eclectic.

Even the communal washing-up tent is photogenic. And we haven't even mentioned the interiors yet, whose bunting, shabby-chic throws, and bed linen have had newspaper travel editors waxing lyrical about this place.

The other founder, Sue, is a dab hand in the kitchen and conjures up homely stews to eat round the campfire on Friday evenings. She also prepares breakfast hampers bursting with pastries, jam, organic bacon, and eggs – delivered to your tent on Saturday mornings.

Everything about Billycan, from the fairy-lit bridge to the beautiful view of the distant castle, is soothing and designed to unravel the city out of your system. This winter they're planting a wild meadow here, so by the time you read this the air will be aflicker with butterflies and heady with the scent of flowers. Book ahead, though; Billycan is deservedly chock-a-block with Boden outdoorsy types and young wannabe pirates. This place deserves to be one of the best campsites in Sussex. And so say all of us.

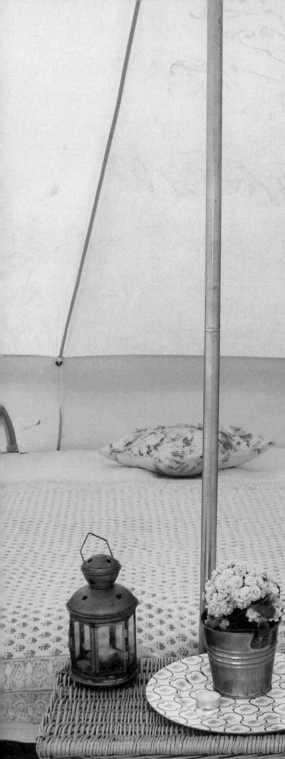

## Billycan Camping

Manor Farm, Tortington, Arundel, West Sussex,
BN18 0BG; www.billycancamping.co.uk

🏕 The 2 tipis (1 sleeps 2 people, the other, 4), 8 bell tents (sleeping 3–5), and 3 yurts (sleeping 4–5) are spread around 7 acres of field, each one individually decked out in shabby-chic style. As there's no electricity, pathways are lit by tea lights. There's face-painting on Saturday mornings, and art classes for the kids. And the kind folk at Billycan will even organise a spa treatment (aromatherapy, Indian head massage, reflexology, or a full-body Swedish massage; £20–£30).

🏕 Big Dave's Bike Hire (£15 per day) is on site – perfect with Arundel close by and the river towpath. Children will love the castle (01903 882173; www.arundelcastle.org) for its weekend events such as jousting or 'have-a-go pirates'. There's Arundel Lido (01903 882404; www.arundel-lido.com) for sweltering days, and Arundel Wetland Centre (01903 883355; see www.wwt.org.uk), where you can take a boat safari through the habitat of rare and endangered species.

🏕 Breakfasts are sorted with your hamper, and there's a great communal BBQ. Should you want more refinement, head into Arundel to Pappardelle (01903 882025; www.pappardelle.co.uk) for freshly cooked Italian cuisine and home-made puddings. And Arundel Brewery (www.arundelbrewery.co.uk) offers a rather nice service – it can deliver its ales to your tent so you needn't go far for a brew.

🏕 Open from May to late September.

🏕 A week's stay in a tipi costs £425 to £600 (depending on the size); a yurt costs £610 to £645; and a bell tent costs £399 to £425. All prices include a hamper and Friday dinner. Shorter breaks are possible too.

# shadow woods

## Shadow Woods

Keepers Barn, Tittlesfold, The Haven, Billingshurst, West Sussex, RH14 9BG; www.woodlandyurting.com

🏕️ Each of the 5 yurts has its own fire pit and sits in a meadow shielded by the forest. There's also a cosy cabin tucked away in the treeline with serene views of the wild meadow, as well as a capacious safari tent. There are compost loos and solar-heated showers.

🏕️ Weald and Downland Open Air Museum (01243 811348; www.wealddown.co.uk) features 6 centuries' worth of preserved rural buildings, has shire horses working the plough, and has resident hens, pigs, and geese.

🏕️ Basic supplies such as eggs as well as home-made delicacies such as quince jelly can be bought on site, and you can pre-order a hamper of organic goodies. For eating out, head to Billingshurst; the Limeburners Arms (01403 782311) offers homely fare in an atmospheric 17th-century cottage.

🏕️ Open from mid April to mid October.

🏕️ Medium yurt (sleeps 2) £260 per week; family yurt and safari tent (both sleep 4) £160 to £380; cabin £150 a night.

From the moment that you drive through its faintly eerie coppice woods, there's something palpably different about Shadow Woods, which nestles in 63 acres of bluebell woodland in the very heart of the Weald Downlands. Fortunately, despite your imagination, there's nothing but welcome calm awaiting you.

There are 100 acres to explore beyond the confines of your elegant yurt or safari tent. And if you thought you were in the middle of nowhere to start with, you'll feel even more gloriously isolated as you wander through the wild meadow: St John's Wort and fleabane flowers glowing brilliantly in the sunshine, and rare butterflies flitting around.

Owner and founder Pom is an ex-film producer of some renown, with modesty to match. She worked with Aussie director Peter Weir on his early films, including classics such as *Picnic at Hanging Rock*. These days she organises candlelit opera evenings in the bluebell woods and ensures that your stay is a peaceful one; for Shadow Woods is a place to regroup and rebalance, whether you're looking for a physical pampering under a spring sky among the bluebells and trees or some woodland edification from a few hours spent with Clive, the resident bushman. Whatever you choose to do, the likelihood is you'll leave feeling a whole lot lighter.

Tipi means 'dwelling' in old Lakota language, though the ones you'll stay in at Big Sky Tipis are Sioux in design. Driving down vernal Sussex lanes to the site is a wonderful culture shock; your first view of the six tents sitting in 22 acres of meadow and woodland is unforgettable and filmic – you almost expect Sitting Bull to pop up with a kola pipe in his mouth at any minute.

The tipis are sufficiently roomy to sleep six and come fully furnished with a comfy double bed, beanbags, and faux-fur rugs on the floor just to add that final element of Crazy Bull authenticity. And, with the fields bordered by ancient woods, you could almost be in Montana, the spiritual home of the Sioux.

The canvas tipis were hand-crafted in Little Creek, Washington state and welcome you in with a womb-like embrace. And when the sun shines, the membrane of the canvas seems to glow with life. But, before we go native on you, what's so special about the place?

Run by the lovely Geoff and Sarah, Big Sky has a laid-back tempo that instantly charms you; nothing seems too much bother and everything has been carefully laid out – from the utensils in a hamper at the foot of your bed to the free-range bacon, sausages, and eggs you can buy from their farm (as well as local venison, game, and fish).

Imagine lounging on a beanbag outside in the evening air as the first stars emerge in the sky, the struts of your tipi striking proudly into the twilit air. The lack of light pollution here makes stargazing such a delight. In days gone by, the original Greenwich Observatory was a mere stroll from the site (at Herstmonceux).

You may not be able to name all the celestial bodies twinkling high above, but you're sure to feel that you've found your own little piece of heaven in a corner of Sussex.

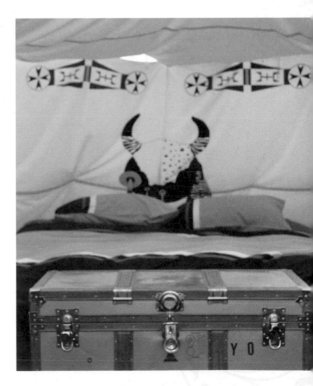

## Big Sky Tipis

Well House, Wartling Road, Wartling, Hailsham,
East Sussex, BN27 1RX
www.bigskytipiholidays.co.uk

🏕 There are 6 tipis, each with individual BBQ.
Campfires are allowed in fire pits as well as a
communal fire to sit round in a powwow. A shower
block up on the hill houses an immaculately clean
washing/shower (piping hot)/loo area that's in
keeping with the natural environment. There's also
a fridge to keep your mescal chilled.

🏕 Big Sky's site is just a 5-minute walk from
Herstmonceux Castle (01323 834444;
www.herstmonceux-castle.com) – similar in style
to Hampton Court – on the grounds of which is the
Observatory Science Centre (01323 832731;
www.the-observatory.org). When there's a celestial
event you can view the stars through the telescopes
there. The typical seaside village of Pevensey Bay is
also just a short drive away. And the 1066 Country
Walk (www.visit1066country.com) passes through
the campsite's ancient Wartling Wood.

🏕 If you're not cooking up the farm's delicious
bacon or venison you might want to pop down
the road to Wartling, where the Lamb Inn (01323
832116; www.lambinnwartling.co.uk) serves up
a mouth-watering menu featuring dishes such
as fresh king scallops served with bacon.

🏕 Open from April through to the end of October.

🏕 There's a minimum 2-night stay per tipi £180 to
£240; and a week's rental costs £300 to £400.

# livingstone lodge

## Livingstone Lodge

Port Lympne Wild Animal Park, Lympne, nr Hythe, Kent, CT21 4PD; www.totallywild.net

🐾 Each of the 9 double, luxury safari tents are complete with open-air veranda, heating, carpets, beds, duvets, and fluffy dressing gowns. There's even a cupboard to hang up clothes and a writing desk, should you wish to pen a letter home. Showers and toilets (including for disabled) are housed in a separate block, but you can always nip there in a fluffy gown. There's a communal canvas-covered lounge with fire pit, aka the 'lapa', for all guests.

🐾 Unlike in Africa, where you eat what you've seen that day – kudu steaks and springbok stew – here, you scoff down locally reared beef and locally fished king prawns. And if you've got room, you might well be finished off by the 'death by chocolate' pudding. Drinks cost extra.

🐾 Open from April to the middle of October.

🐾 Prices start from £119 per person per night sharing; kids (9 to 14 years) sharing cost £120; no children under 9 are allowed. The price does include a 3-course dinner and breakfast. And just the sunrises are worth it.

Dawn. A misty sun rises over the marsh. The good morning 'roar' of an ex-Zimbabwean game ranger signals coffee and time to get up – a call from the wild that is the start of your extraordinary journey across the teaming plains of this out-of-Africa experience.

Overlooking the Romney Marshes along the Kentish coast is the 100-acre Port Lympne Wild Animal Park. John Aspinall, a once notorious gambler and wildlife enthusiast, won the park in a card game and then stocked the place with his favourite Indian and African wildlife. His theory – give animals enough space and a close proximity to their natural patch and they will breed. His proof – restocking the Gobi Desert with the once-extinct wild horses from his park.

What the park trust is trying to do in terms of breeding is ambitious. You can't help but gulp when you learn that of the 60,000 black rhino that used to roam the African continent fewer than 3,000 are left. And, what's more, the largest breeding herd outside of their home territory is right here at Port Lympne.

En route to your luxury pit stop for the night, you rock and roll through the park in a beast of an open-sided 4x4. On the way you see eland, zebra, wildebeest, and, if you're lucky, Sebastian the giraffe, who might well deposit a two-metre-long dollop of dribble in your lap.

The lodge itself – a replica of the swish tented camps of Africa – has nine enormous luxury canvas tents on stilts, perched atop a hill, overlooking vast expanses of marshy countryside and the English Channel. Once you're settled in, join the other guests for pre-dinner drinks in the 'lapa' – a canvas lounge with rustic furniture and open fire. Chat or just watch hungrily as a traditional feast is prepared before you.

Get an early night in readiness for the pre-dawn call; that's if you're not woken before by the grunts and snorts of animals just outside.

white horse
gypsy caravan

Clip-clopping through the picture-perfect Pewscy Vale in a gypsy caravan – life on the open road doesn't get much better than this.

When you first clamber up the wooden steps and through the door of this traditional vardo, you'll be amazed at how tiny it is. It seems sacrilegious to mess it all up with your luggage and trappings, which look so garish against the delicate hand-painted wood and dainty gingham curtains. While there's no denying it's a squeeze, stow things away and suddenly you'll find that you're in the Tardis.

Getting your trusty steed tacked up, ready for the road, is not as speedy as a car's mirror-signal-manoeuvre, but hearing the creak of the wooden wheels and the clop of the horse's hooves, you'll soon be rocking into chillsville.

Plodding along the open road in your own house-on-wheels, your horse is doing all the hard graft so you can relax. Do remember to take it in turns to hold the reins and wave to passers-by. You can even have a go at bareback-riding, with the groom's approval.

The itinerary is set in stone so that both you and the horse can get to certain points at specific times for rest, relaxation, or running around – especially the predestined overnight camping spot. Despite the fixed nature of the route, you won't feel tied down at all. Simply spend your three days ambling through White Horse, stone-, and crop-circle country; there's something special afoot here. This manifests most strikingly at night when you're camped in an open field with a stream trickling nearby.

The thoughtful folks at White Horse Gypsy Caravan HQ provide you with a real live groom, who is as hands-on, or -off, as you want, but appears like a lucky charm within minutes of any call for assistance.

The only drawback is that you do have to hand back your mighty steed and temporary home. Then, it's a case of shifting up a gear or two to return to the pace of normal life.

## White Horse Gypsy Caravan

Kate's Cottage, Alton Priors, Marlborough,
Wiltshire, SN8 4JX
www.whitehorsegypsycaravans.co.uk

🌢 Booking is essential as this is the only hireable horse-drawn gypsy caravan in England. A pull-out bed at the back of the caravan sleeps 2 adults and there's room on the floor for a mattress for small ones. A vast array of cosy bedding is stashed away. There's a 2-ring gas stove for basic cooking and kettle-boiling, as well as a small electric light. Beneath the caravan you'll find all you need for a BBQ, from charcoal to pans. The service is outstanding, as a cool bag is provided and your groom will drop off newly frozen ice blocks – twice a day if necessary. Your horse is also provided with a bucket, so don't forget to give Tom or Molly plenty of water. If you're wondering about ablutions, you have access to a bathroom at base camp on the first and last night, and there's a portaloo awaiting you in the field on night 2. At other times of day, if you're not near a pub, well, you're in the countryside – bushes abound.

🌢 The itinerary is based around family-friendly pubs with good grub, in beautiful country settings. You'll visit the Barge Inn at Honeystreet (01672 851705; www.the-barge-inn.com), a 10-minute walk from base camp. Next stop Marden, followed by the Seven Stars at Bottlesford (01672 851325; www.thesevenstars.co.uk) and finally it's the Woodbridge at North Newnton (01980 630266; www.thewoodbridgeinn.co.uk). There are no shops en route, but if you need something, ring Polly or her groom and they'll deliver it at the next stop.

🌢 Open from May to October.

🌢 The price is £450 for 3 days (starting on a Friday or on a Tuesday).

For most of the year there aren't any turkeys in Turkey Creek, and even though you're just over the road from the Thames towpath, the creek isn't that obvious either; nevertheless, it's a fabulous place to relax with friends or family.

The set-up here is camping within a shady wood; you can choose from a rustic bell tent, tipi, or yurt for your temporary dwelling. There's even a log cabin for those who'd prefer not to brave any elements at all.

The owners, Anni and Charles, are very keen to make campers feel welcome and relaxed, and generally like they've been transported to a world away from the trappings of modern life. There's no TV common room with an Xbox here. Instead, the orders of the day are making fires, sitting by fires, cooking on fires, and enjoying the freedom of the woodland in between.

And if anything about this place is a talking point it's the compost loos, housed in a *Hansel and Gretel*-style wooden chalet, along a little track leading deeper into the trees.

Young campers can horse around on the recycled tyre 'horse swing' or clamber up the hand-made wooden climbing frame, and there are opportunities aplenty for making dens or playing outdoor games. Then, there are resident dogs to stroke and goats to admire, and who doesn't enjoy collecting

freshly laid eggs from the chicken coop? Or if you just want to sit back and read, there's plenty of room for that too.

## Turkey Creek

Westmoor Farm, Buckland Road, Bampton,
Oxfordshire, OX18 2AA
www.turkeycreek.co.uk

🏕️ A bell tent, a tipi, a yurt, and a log cabin, with space for your own tents if you need extra accommodation. All glamping tents have either a chimenea or wood-burner inside. There are gas BBQs; all cooking equipment is supplied – just bring your food. Beds are futons or camp beds, complete with all bedding. The free hot showers and compost loos are all housed in a wooden A-frame chalet at the edge of the wood. Ice-block freezing is available.

🏕️ Turkey Creek is only a few minutes from the Thames towpath (across a main road). Starting at nearby Tadpole Bridge you can walk all the way to Lechlade (11 miles), or just sit and watch people messing about in boats. Turkey Creek has its own rubber dinghy and outboard motor, though it's best to arrange hiring this in advance.

🏕️ The village of Bampton has a good local butcher, a small supermarket and newsagent, and a coffee shop. At Tadpole Bridge, there's the award-winning Trout Inn (01367 870382; www.trout-inn.co.uk), and there's the Clanfield Tavern (01367 810223; www.clanfieldtavern.com) in Clanfield; both pubs serve good food. The Snooty Mehmaan (01367 242260; www.thesnootymehmaan.co.uk), the local Indian restaurant in Faringdon, will even deliver spicy delights to the flaps of your tent.

🏕️ Open all year.

🏕️ The bell tent, tipi, yurt, and log cabin cost £65 per night (each sleeps up to 2 adults and 2 children).

Abbey Home Farm is not just a beautiful place – it is a living expression of one family's passion. There are quite definitely no food miles here, and the organic label is far from a gimmick or token gesture; this is a farm that has always been at the forefront of the organic farming movement. And it's truly exciting (and delicious, too) to experience it for yourself.

A selection of pitches is scattered around the 1,500 acres of Soil Association–certified organic farm. You can, if you prefer, bring your own tent and pitch it in the Green Field site, sheltered by the mystical, ancient oaks.

But the no-hassle option is to book one of the yurt sites. These plots are quite magical and they camouflage perfectly into the surrounding landscape. If the kids do get lost in the greenery of it all, remind them to just look to the skyline and search for the brightly painted totem pole nearby. And the signs for the compost loos. And the recycling station. And the sculpture in the tree.

New couple-only additions to the farm's fold are a shepherd's hut, and another hut by the pond – a truly peaceful spot. Both sleep two and are available for romance and rekindling of love all year, with mattresses, wood-burner, and firewood thrown in.

What you'll get from this camping experience, as well as peace and quiet and the chance to sit in a leafy clearing around a campfire, is a real sense of perspective on life. Organic living isn't just a dream here; it has actually become a reality.

## Abbey Home Farm

Burford Road, Cirencester, Gloucestershire, GL7 5HF
www.theorganicfarmshop.co.uk

🌿 The 4-yurt camp (for groups of family and friends; sleeps up to 18) is only a 5-minute walk from the farm shop. The yurts are unfurnished but have carpets and there are mattresses to sling on the floor, whenever the mood takes you. The main yurt has a wood-burner and gas stove, but it's more fun to cook on the open fire in the middle of the camp. The single yurt is as well equipped, sleeps up to 5, and is 20 minutes from the café. Compost loos are tucked away in leafy clearings and timed water-squirters let you wash your hands without waste. The recycling station is a work of art (literally).

🌿 You are in Roman-remains territory, and Chedworth Villa (www.chedworthromanvilla.com) is less than 10 minutes away by car and has some fantastic mosaics. The Corinium Museum in Cirencester (01285 655611) has recently been renovated, with interactive displays and the opportunity to dress up as a Roman soldier. You're also on the edge of the Cotswolds, with Cheltenham and Stow-on-the-Wold within half-an-hour's drive.

🌿 Don't bring any food with you, just buy it here. The farm shop and café produce deliciousness: milk and meat, fruit and veg, cakes, and even Sunday lunch. You can walk to the Village Pub in Barnsley (01285 740421; www.thevillagepub.co.uk) if you fancy something a bit more upmarket.

🌿 Open from Easter to October for yurts; the huts are open all year.

🌿 The 4-yurt camp costs £975 for a week or £550 for a long weekend. The single yurt, shepherd's hut, and hut each cost £100 for 2 nights (minimum stay).

woodland tipi
and yurts

There's nothing to suggest, as you turn off the road and head up the drive of Woodlands Farm, that you're mere metres from not just another glampsite, but a whole little village of happy glamping. However, turn left along a path through the woods and first one then another yurt begin to emerge from among the trees.

A high tarp covers dinner tables decked with tiny vases of freshly cut wild flowers; rope ladders and swings hang from high branches; while on the wall of a wooden shelter a row of colourful water bottles begs to have an arty photo taken of it.

And rightly so, because everything about this site bears the touch of its owner, Julia, who trained as an artist. The compost loos are things of beauty, bunting flaps jauntily in the breeze, and exotic tea-light lamps hang from rafters. As you continue through the wood along the track (originally created for training huskies), a bakehouse and its clay oven heave into view (so definitely bring pizza ingredients).

Beyond the bakehouse are the unmistakable peaks of Sioux-inspired tipis – like the yurts, each one has plenty of space around it in which to breathe, and a hammock stretched between trees for maximum chilling. Inside, real beds and low furniture encourage guests to relax further. And should the sun not blaze, warmth is supplied by wood-burning stoves (in the yurts) and chimeneas (in the tipis). The site has its own signposted woodland path down to nearby Hoarwithy with its pub and Italianate church. In spring, however, there's a very good chance you'll be stopped in your tracks by the glories of the bluebell wood, so be sure to pack those watercolours.

## Woodland Tipi and Yurts

Woodlands Farm, Little Dewchurch, Herefordshire,
HR2 6QD; www.woodlandtipis.co.uk

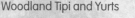 There are 4 tipis and 4 yurts, while the extensive
facilities run to 3 flushing toilets, 3 compost loos,
3 showers, a lovely little bathroom, and 2 fully
equipped kitchens. Each tipi and yurt also has its
own fridge-freezer. There is a fire pit by each tipi and
yurt (firewood is provided for the wood-burners and
chimeneas). Children can make dens in the woods,
climb on ladders hanging from trees, and play in the
sandpit and the playhouse tipi. Bread and milk are
available for sale on site. The nearest shop is a Londis
in Wormelow (5 miles). There's an extra kitchen hut
with 2 extra compost loos, and extra showers are
planned for 2011.

Hereford Cathedral (www.herefordcathedral.
org) contains the world-renowned medieval Mappa
Mundi and Chained Library, while the Forest of Dean
(www.visitforestofdean.co.uk) is home to cycle
trails, woodland thrills, a huge playground,
llama-trekking, and much more besides.

The Cottage of Content pub (01432 840242;
www.cottageofcontent.co.uk) in Carey, a 5-minute
drive away, serves excellent food. And the local farm
shop Carey Organics (veg, fruit, meat, cider; 01432
840959; www.whitethornfarm.co.uk) will even
deliver to your woodland dwelling.

Open from early April to late September.

One week prices in high season are: tipi (sleeps 5)
£650; yurt (sleeps 5) £680; and large yurt (sleeps 7)
£700. Shorter breaks are also available outside high
season (weekend rates start from £200).

# tipi adventure

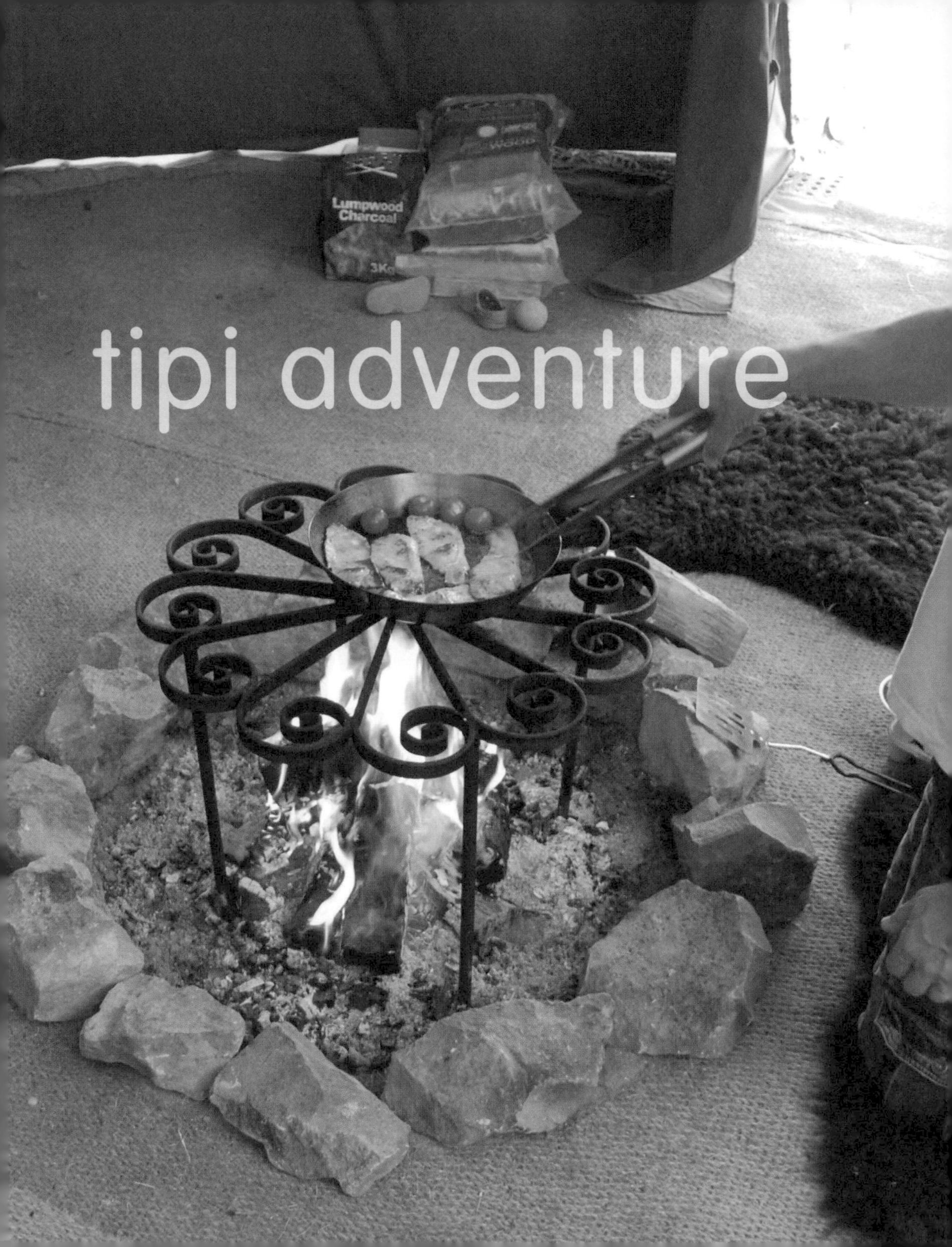

There's an air of the great North American wilderness about this particular camping experience. You clamber aboard an Old Town open canoe and paddle down-river to your destination – a Native American-style tipi sitting majestically on the banks of the water. Except the Mississippi this ain't – you're on the River Wye in stunning Herefordshire country.

This is a professional set-up. It has to be, as you need a health and safety chat before you can go on the river. The Tipi Adventure team is a friendly and relaxed one and happy to help with anything you may have forgotten (a fully charged mobile phone is a compulsory accessory for such eventualities, and for arranging to be picked up). After wriggling into your life jacket you, and your picnic, are put into a canoe, then on to the water at an agreed spot (some people want to canoe all day, others for just a couple of hours), while any luggage is driven to the tipi to await your arrival. It's all very civilised.

You can then take your time paddling downstream, stopping at the river's edge for lunch… and trying to avoid the (extremely serious) fishermen posted randomly along the river bank. It's great fun cutting through the water at whatever pace you want to set, quacking at ducks, and learning from other canoeists' mistakes (the odd capsizing or two

have been known to happen). And just when you think you can't possibly paddle any further, you're encouraged onwards by the sight of tipi poles peeking out behind the bend in the river. Perfect timing.

It's exciting to bale out of the canoe, clamber up the bank, and run across the field to your tipi and find your belongings waiting inside. So, it must be time to light a fire (and hang any soggy clothing off the guy ropes) and then flop, cook, explore the river bank, or quench that thirst you've built up.

The joy of these tipis is their location: remote and secret. There's barely any light

pollution, so stargazing on a clear night is the main attraction, as well as listening to the crackling of the campfire (and fellow tipi-dwellers doing exactly the same). Oh, and you'll be glad that you stocked up on marshmallows at base camp.; nothing like a chargrilled bit of stickiness to keep the blood sugar levels up for the next day's activity.

Waking up to the sound of river-bird song, or a fish leaping out of the water, is wonderful. It really is that rural here. And eating bacon that you've just fried over the fire pit is a great way to set you up for the day's adventure. Before you hop back into the canoe, do pack up all your belongings, which you'll be reunited with back at base camp.

It's such a serene way to start the day, once again paddling through the clear water… Actually, scratch that – it's time to get competitive and catch up with (or get a good headstart on) your tipi neighbours of last night to see who can get to the New Harp Inn at Hoarwithy first for lunch.

At some stage you'll meet the Tipi Adventure driver at a pre-arranged place to load your canoe on to the trailer before clambering into the minibus. Sitting there, smelling of bonfire smoke, you'll take one last glance back at that stunning river and, no doubt, wish you'd paddled that bit further.

## Tipi Adventure

Whitehall Farm, Hampton Bishop, Herefordshire, HR1 4LD
www.tipiadventure.co.uk

🏕️ Campfires are allowed inside and outside of the tipis, which are pitched in clusters of 2 or 3 on the banks of the river. Each tipi is fully equipped with all the bedding and cooking equipment that you'll need. All you have to bring is food. At base camp you're issued with a cool box and ice blocks, and there's a tuck shop for stocking up on campfire essentials – including marshmallows. Behind the tipis there are shared portaloos with integrated washbasins. There are no proper showering facilities, which is a tad disappointing, but no real hardship for a weekend.

🏕️ Everyone tends to stay on site. But at the end of your adventure, pay a visit to the Hereford Cider Museum (www.cidermuseum.co.uk) or Westons Cider (www.westons-cider.co.uk) at Much Marcle to quench that canoeing thirst.

🏕️ Stock up on food before you reach base camp. The nearby village of Fownhope has an excellent butcher and convenience shop. The team will show you where good pubs and refreshment stops are on the map. If you want lunch before checking in at basecamp, the Bunch of Carrots (01432 870237; www.bunch-of-carrots.co.uk) at Hampton Bishop serves good food. En route, the New Harp Inn (01432 840900; www.thenewharpinn.co.uk) at Hoarwithy serves excellent gastropub food. The Hope and Anchor (01989 563003; www.hopeandanchorross.com) at Ross-on-Wye is a favourite at the end of the adventure.

🏕️ Open from the start of April to early October.

🏕️ Tipi (sleeps 7) £150 to 230 per night (depending on the season), plus £45 per canoe (seats 3 adults or 2 adults and 2 children).

Do you and your kids feel like having a little TLC? Here's a place to cocoon your family in an idyllic world – just for a weekend. And it's a kids' (big and small) Utopia: a tempting combination of tents and food – all enclosed in a cosy Victorian walled garden.

Talton Lodge has the ultimate secret garden that you can just disappear into. When the latched wooden gate is opened you'll be sure to gasp with excitement at the sight in front of you (it's rather like the beginning of a theme park advert, but without the schmaltz).

The campsite is in a Victorian red-brick walled garden, with everything you'd expect – veggie patches, raspberry bushes, chicken coops, an orchard – all topped off with a babbling brook. You'll find tipis, yurts, and a pavilion (for all your ablutions), surrounded by all the trappings of self-sufficiency, from soft fruit to hand-reared heavenly hog.

The Norwegian tipi on the lawn is massive (vast enough to hold a wedding for 65 guests). And across the gravel path you'll find a traditionally decorated Mongolian yurt. Behind the cast-iron gates, just beyond the wall, you'll also be able to glimpse a traditional North American tipi.

The outdoors here is paradise; kids can run in and out of trees and tents, and there are a further 20 acres surrounding this. Throw in

Talton's owner Olivia, who dishes up delicious three-course dinners – you'd be mad not to take advantage of her cooking during your stay – and you won't be able to help feeling completely relaxed at this heavenly place.

## Talton Lodge

Newbold-on-Stour, Warwickshire, CV37 8UB
www.taltonlodge.co.uk

🏕 There are 4 sleeping 'tents' (2 tipis and 2 yurts) in the walled garden. There's also a barn, which easily sleeps 6, or 8 if needed. Whether you opt for a tipi or one of the hand-painted yurts, you'll be snug as a bug; there are wood-burners in each one. The huge Norwegian tipi acts as a living and dining space, while the 'pavilion' houses showers, loos, and kitchen.

🏕 If you want to explore further than the woods on site, there are cycle paths galore in this beautiful part of Warwickshire. For those who feel the need to get into a car, Warwick Castle (08712 652000; www.warwick-castle.co.uk) has ramparts, battles... and even a gift shop.

🏕 Olivia provides home-produced free-range eggs, bread, preserves, sausages, and ham, plus veg and fruit (in season). Buy one of her breakfast boxes, cook melt-in-the-mouth sausages for the kids' tea, get them tucked up, and then ask Olivia to serve you a 3-course dinner. Plus, there are 2 good pubs in the village: the White Hart (01789 450205) and the Bird in Hand (01789 450253).

🏕 Open from April to October.

🏕 Prices per person per night are £50 for stays at weekends and £35 on weekdays. Discounts are available for longer stays.

There's something undeniably enchanting about Jollydays, a relatively new site set up in 2009 by husband-and-wife team Christian and Carolyn Van Outersterp. Having previously masterminded London's stylish bar/restaurant and discreet celebrity hang-out CVO Firevault, the couple opted to quit the city rat race and fulfil their dream of creating a better lifestyle for their family.

The result is a sustainable campsite in the middle of a wood just 20 minutes from the historic centre of York. Comprised entirely of generously spaced pre-constructed bell tents, luxury lodge tents, and de luxe tents, this 200-acre woodland site casts a calming spell on you as soon as you enter its leafy embrace.

Cars are parked off site to minimise any disruption, and the tents are lovingly decorated with lots of colourful, retro touches like funky furniture, bunting, and ornaments. They're fully equipped, of course, with BBQs, picnic benches, wood-burners, and proper beds; the de luxe tents have en suite showers, loos, and kitchens. You'll even find cool boxes, daily ice packs, loo roll, and all you need for washing up.

A 'cake' tent full of home-made goodies and a communal campfire serve as public areas, and the Van Outersterps can arrange pretty much anything for you, from archery and champagne picnics to woodcraft lessons.

And if you venture outside the confines of this magical site, prepare to be dazzled by a whole clutch of places to explore, including two fantastic national parks, several Areas of Outstanding Natural Beauty, a stunning heritage coastline, and, of course, bewitching York, with its impressive wealth of attractions and charming atmosphere.

## Jollydays

Village Farm, Scrayingham, North Yorkshire, YO41 1JD
www.jollydaysluxurycamping.co.uk

🐚 The 20 pre-erected tents (7 bell, 9 luxury lodge, and 4 de luxe) are spread spaciously over 200 acres of woodland. There are communal showers and toilets for the bell tents: 6 powerful showers and 2 washing-up areas. De luxe and lodge tents have their own facilities. A communal campfire is lit every evening. The reception tent has tea and home-made cakes ('honesty' box), and a small shop sells everything from charcoal to vintage cushions.

🐚 If the rope swings and hammocks aren't keeping you (or your lot) entertained, you could always zip over to the high wires of Go Ape (08456 439215; www.goape.co.uk) in Dalby Forest; or check out Flamingo Land (www.flamingoland.co.uk), a theme park, resort, and zoo. Castle Howard (01653 648333; www.castlehoward.co.uk) is a magnificent 18th-century residence set within a spectacular landscape; while York Maze (01904 607341; www. yorkmaze.com) is a lot of fun in the summertime.

🐚 The Balloon Tree Farm Shop and Café (01759 373023; www.theballoontree.co.uk) at Gate Helmsley sells its own home-grown fruit and veg, farm-reared meat, and excellent cakes. The Stone Trough Inn (01653 618713; www.stonetroughinn. co.uk) at Kirkham Abbey is an award-winning English pub, serving a variety of Yorkshire ales. But for something further afield and a bit special, book a table at the Michelin-starred Harome's Star Inn (01439 770397; www.thestaratharome.co.uk).

🐚 Open from mid March through to 2nd January.

🐚 Prices depend on the tent you choose and how long you stay. A week in a bell tent costs £470 to £660, luxury lodge tent £585 to £900, and de luxe £670 to £990; weekend breaks are £275 to £575.

la rosa

Day-Glo carnival psychedelia is the order of the day at La Rosa, where camping and the world of kitsch go colourfully and surreally hand in hand. The nine themed vintage caravans are fun, quirky, and comfy; but they are definitely not what you'd call luxurious. Old-fashioned eiderdowns and wood-burning stoves will keep you warm and cosy, but don't come expecting any mod cons.

Candlelight, lanterns, and campfires replace electricity, adding to the romantic – almost magical – atmosphere, while a compost loo, cowshed showers, open-air bath, and enamel washstands complete the low environmental-impact facilities. The site is surrounded by the North Yorkshire Moors National Park's forest, with views from the lower field over beautiful, expansive moorland; and the folks at La Rosa have made every effort to run the site in harmony with this surrounding Area of Outstanding Natural Beauty.

Each trailer has its own theme. Uncover Romany culture in Tinkers' Trailer, or bow to The King in the American-style Elvis trailer. Go on a night's Seventies Safari, or on a trip with Barbara Cartland on acid in Psycho Candy. And did we mention the circus big top? This large communal tent, built by a real circus actor, sits in a grove in the top field surrounded by vintage 1920s campervans.

Whichever world you choose to make your own for the night, you'll never have stayed anywhere quite like this before.

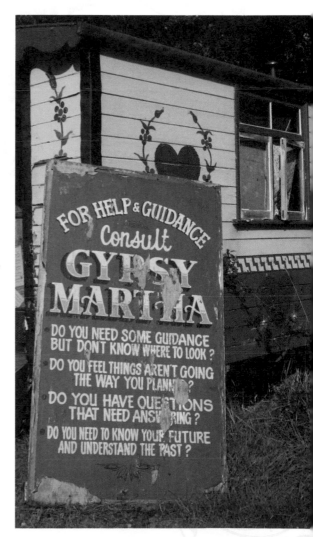

## La Rosa Campsite Extraordinaire

*Murk Esk Cottage, Goathland, Whitby, North Yorkshire, YO22 5AS; www.larosa.co.uk*

🐚 A total of 9 individually themed vintage caravans are tucked within this woodland-enclosed site. You'll find showers in the old milking parlour, and a compost loo in a shepherd's hut disguised as a fortune-teller's booth. There's a big top circus tent stuffed with tea sets, dressing-up clothes, and games; a tipi; and an old-fashioned 'honesty' sweet shop completes the rather unusual facilities. Plus, there are communal campfires.

🐚 Nearby Goathland is famous for being not only the backdrop to the popular *Heartbeat* TV series, but also Hogwarts station in the Harry Potter films. Hop on board one of the steam or diesel locomotives of the North Yorkshire Moors Railway (01751 472508; www.nymr.co.uk) to reach the seaside town of Whitby, or Pickering in the other direction.

🐚 You can walk to one of England's oldest (and most eccentric?) pubs, the Birch Hall Inn (01947 896245) in Beckhole; it serves 'Beckhole Butties' along with a range of local microbrews.

🐚 Open May to September, weekends only.

🐚 Price per caravan per night is £60 (most sleep 2 adults, some can also squeeze in a couple of kids), including bedding, gas, candles, and firewood.

# dolphinholme

## Dolphinholme House Farm

Dolphinholme, Lancaster, Lancashire, LA2 9DJ; www.featherdown.co.uk

🐾 Each of the 7 tents is fully equipped with everything you might need. Lighting is by oil lamp and candles – there's no electricity. The 'honesty' shop is always open and is well stocked with lots of locally sourced deliciousness.

🐾 There are ponies, hens, pigs, goats, rabbits, and guinea pigs – so lots of petting to be done. There's onsite bike hire (bring your helmets) and tours of the farm, with trails and footpaths. Further afield, picnic at Abbeystead reservoir, fish at Wyreside Lakes (01524 792093), or ride at the Bay Horse School of Equitation at Forton (01524 791154).

🐾 At Wallings Farm near Cockerham (01524 793781; www.wallingsfarm.co.uk) there's an ice-cream parlour as well as a coffee shop and a good restaurant. The Fleece Inn (01524 791233; www.thefleeceinndolphinholme.co.uk) in Dolphinholme serves hearty pub grub while the Bay Horse (01524 791204; www.bayhorseinn.com) in Forton offers gastropub fare.

🐾 Open from Easter until late October.

🐾 Tents cost £435 to £845 for a week, £225 to £539 for a 4-night midweek stay, and £279 to £589 for a weekend.

Dolphinholme House Farm has been in John Gorst's family since the 1930s, sitting at the western edge of the Trough of Bowland, a truly beautiful part of the world, just south of the Lake District. Seven spacious and very comfortable 'tents' – they have raised wooden floors and beds with mattresses, pillows, and even duvets – are set out on the edge of 35 acres of woodland overlooking a 10-acre field. The River Wyre, fringed by a line of trees at the bottom of the field, seems to be the only thing rushing by in this peaceful spot.

The emphasis at this working goat dairy farm is on good old-fashioned fun, and the site offers plenty of opportunities for this – swimming, paddling, and pottering around with fishing nets in the river, or just picnicking on its banks, climbing trees, running about in the fields, and climbing on bales of hay. And you can pet more than goats here; there are animals of all shapes and sizes.

If your inner chef is calling, opt for a 'slow food' supper, where all the ingredients and equipment for your campfire stew or soup are provided. Then, come the end of the day, you can enjoy the simple pleasures of stories around the campfire or games by candlelight.

Campers can also learn about farm life and where food comes from by helping with the milking (the farm makes its own goats' cheese), gathering eggs from the henhouse, or rolling up your sleeves to pitch in at making pizza or bread in the traditional wood-fired oven.

long valley
yurts

Tucked away on the quieter western shore of Lake Windermere you'll find the delightful rambling estate of Wray Castle, once the summer abode of a young Beatrix Potter. Nearly 50 years ago the National Trust turned the grounds into what is now one of Cumbria's loveliest campsites with pitches in fields, pitches (and pods) in woods, and pitches right on the lake shore – it's a real somewhere-for-everyone kind of place. Nevertheless, there was something missing. 'What about', cried people who wanted to stay there in a yurt or a bell tent, 'people who want to stay there in a yurt or a bell tent?'

Now, with the arrival of Long Valley Yurts, that cry has been answered. In a field bordered on one side by trees and the curiously spelled Blelham Beck, and just beyond a brand new facilities block, sit two yurts and three bell tents awaiting your indulgence.

It's a widely held belief – based, it must be said, on nothing more tangible than empirical evidence and historical documentation – that yurts are a form of dwelling emanating from the Central Asian steppe (where they are sometimes known as gers) rather than, say, North Africa. One must therefore congratulate the good people at Long Valley on the inspirational brainwave that led them to decorate the yurts here as if they were from Morocco. The furniture, rugs, and even the lanterns conjure up a vision of old Marrakech. There's also a fully equipped kitchen in which visitors can bang out some falafels to accompany their tabouleh and hummus. It's post-modernism given a jokey twist. 'Was Genghis Khan', they appear to be asking, 'actually an African?'

What we can be sure of is that North Africa is, as a rule, hotter than Cumbria, so to redress the balance, extra warmth comes courtesy of a wood-burning stove for which firewood and kindling is provided. Should it rain, you can curl up smugly snug with your

nearest and dearest or rifle through the games chest and beat them into a pulp at Monopoly or Battleships. And when bedtime comes, everyone can forget those arguments about which player would have won first prize in the beauty contest, and drift off to sleep gazing up through the skylight at the constellations above.

But it's not all lying back and thinking of Orion. The owners are more than happy to organise a whole host of activities to get your teeth into (literally, in the case of the bushcraft course). Trained instructors will take you rock-climbing, abseiling, ghyll-scrambling, mountain walking, mountain-biking, Ray Mears-ing, or, perhaps most excitingly, canoeing – you can paddle from right outside your front door, down the Blelham, and out on to Lake Windermere itself.

England's largest lake is, naturally, a Mecca for lovers of all kinds of aquatic pastimes, with local companies offering a chance to try out sailing, water-skiing, and windsurfing (www.lakesleisure.org.uk). Or, if that's all a bit too energetic-sounding, you can always hop on one of the many cruisers (www.windermere-lakecruises.co.uk) that chug remorselessly back and forth over the water.

Long Valley Yurts also has bell tents and yurts at two other sites in the Lake District:

Great Langdale (beneath the mighty Langdale Pikes) and Borrowdale (near the pretty hamlet of Grange). But, if your heart is set on Low Wray, and you prefer your accommodation of the pointy variety, your luck's still in: 4 Winds Lakeland Tipis (www.4windslakelandtipis.co.uk) has set up a number of the iconic conical tents in the other half of the bell tent/yurt field, creating a whole community of alternative outdoor dwellers.

## Long Valley Yurts

Low Wray National Trust Campsite, Ambleside,
Cumbria, LA22 0JA
www.long-valley-yurts.co.uk

🐚 The 2 yurts and 3 bell tents each sleep up to 5
(1 double, 2 singles, and 1 blow-up mattress), and all
bed linen is supplied. A fully equipped kitchen has gas
hobs and grill, while lighting and fairy lights are
solar-powered. Numerous showers and loos are but
a step away. An onsite adventure playground will
keep the kids entertained for hours, while a tiny shop
will tide you over if you've forgotten something.

🐚 If you're after something other than that
provided by Long Valley Yurts, seek out Grizedale
Forest (see www.forestry.gov.uk) for some buzz *à la
bicyclette*, from the most family-friendly tracks to
the taxing North Face Trail. Grizedale Mountain Bikes
(01229 860369; www.grizedalemountainbikes.co.
uk) will happily hire you a bike. The World of Beatrix
Potter (www.hop-skip-jump.com) is over the other
side of the lake, at Bowness; not to be confused with
the author's house, Hilltop (01539 436269; see
www.nationaltrust.org.uk) at Near Sawrey, which is
much closer and permanently besieged by Japanese
tourists who simply cannot get enough of Peter
Rabbit, Mrs Tiggy-Winkle, et al.

🐚 The Drunken Duck Inn (01539 436347; www.
drunkenduckinn.co.uk) has a reputation for serving
some of the best pub food in Britain, and is only a
couple of miles away. Lucy's of Ambleside (01539
432288; www.lucysofambleside.co.uk) is a deli with
its own café/restaurant and sells delicious, if hardly
inexpensive, ingredients for your camp nosh-fest.

🐚 Open from late March to early November.

🐚 A yurt's weekly rental is £385 to £460, with
midweek breaks and weekends costing £285 to
£325. Bell tents cost £355 to £395 for a week and
£235 to £255 for a weekend or midweek stay.

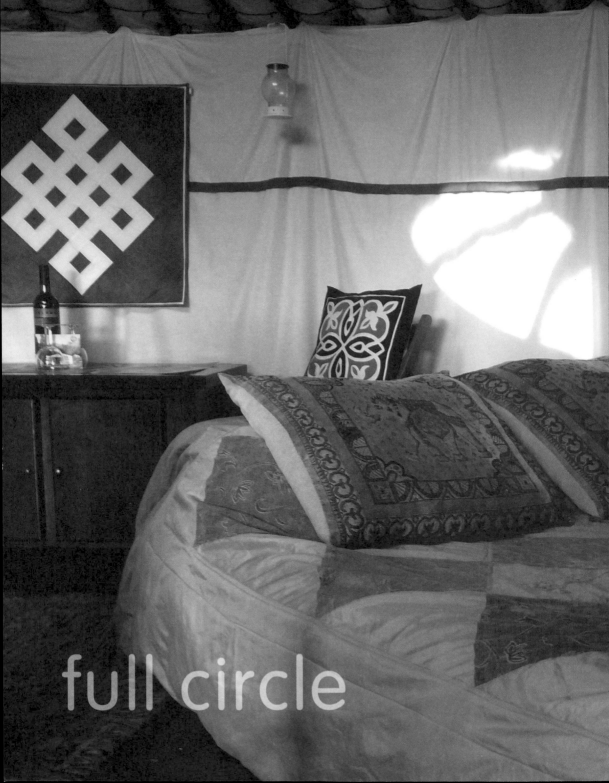

full circle

If only Wordsworth had held on another 160-odd years, then instead of mooning over daffodils, vales, hills, and the like, he could have written impassioned paeans to that most sumptuous of mobile dwelling places, the yurt. The five kept by Full Circle are high on a hill, just a sonnet or two from the house in which the poet lived for the latter half of his life, and come with views that are wont to inspire anyone to feats of high wordsmithery.

And it's the very Mongolianness of the yurts that charms and entrances guests. Hand-crafted in Ulaanbaatar, each is made from five layers of fabric to keep you cool when it's hot and cosy when the nights draw in. It's good to know that past guests have stayed warm and toasty even when there was deep snow and temperatures plummeted below zero.

Inside, traditional Mongolian decorations add that extra soupçon of steppe life. And on the rug-covered wooden floor there's a big double bed and two singles. You can rustle up your favourite scran on a cast-iron, double gas hob in a tiled kitchen area (or on the BBQ), challenge all comers to one of the board games, or curl up with a book from your yurt's private collection. Your green sensibilities will tingle at the discovery that the lighting inside is solar-powered and your bottle of 'welcome to the yurt' wine is organic.

If you should make it beyond your picnic-friendly decking, the grounds of Rydal Hall – a retreat centre on whose estate the yurts stand – are yours to explore. That means 30 acres of woods, an adventure playground, a beck tumbling down a waterfall, formal Edwardian gardens, and a tea shop.

But you might just prefer to lie back in your hammock, gaze out over fells Loughrigg and Wansfell Pike, and muse, with Wordsworth, that yurt 'has not anything to show more fair'.

## Full Circle

Rydal Hall, Rydal, Ambleside, Cumbria, LA22 9LX
www.lake-district-yurts.co.uk

🐚 Each of the 5 yurts sleep up to 6 – 1 double bed, 2 singles (all linen supplied), and floor room for 2 more. There are braziers for fires outside, and wood-burning stoves and ovens inside (all wood provided). There's a brand new hydroelectric-powered loo and shower block; drinking water comes straight off the fell so tastes particularly sweet; and there's a laundry room too. The loos and showers are a short walk away, but down a steep hill.

🐚 Wordsworth acolytes should make a beeline for his old residence Rydal Mount and its tea room (01539 433002; www.rydalmount.co.uk). The lovely Coffin Trail passes through the grounds on its way to Grasmere. And discounted passes to the Langdale Hotel's (www.langdale.co.uk) spa are available from the campsite owners (Ben and Sue). Ben also does wild swimming and walking tours.

🐚 Give one or both of Ambleside's 2 art house cinema-restaurants (one is vegetarian) a whirl (www.fellinisambleside.com; www.zeffirellis.com). Café-cum-restaurant-cum-deli Lucy's of Ambleside (01539 432288; www.lucysofambleside.co.uk) also comes highly recommended.

🐚 Open all year.

🐚 Yurts cost £495 a week; a 3-night weekend/ 4-night midweek costs £295. Those arriving by public transport get a 10 per cent discount.

# pot-a-doodle do

## Pot-a-Doodle Do

Borewell Farm, Scremerston, Berwick-upon-Tweed, Northumberland, TD15 2RJ; www.northumbrianwigwams.com

🏕️ Choose from 1 of the 20 wooden wigwams and 3 yurts scattered around this coastal site. Facilities-wise, there's a well-equipped kitchen, onsite shop, laundry room, free showers, art centre, and children's play area.

🏕️ Head to Holy Island's Lindisfarne Castle, the abbey, or tea shops; just mind the tides! Or cruise to the Farne Islands for the unforgettable sight and sound of 150,000 birds. Boats leave regularly from Seahouses.

🏕️ The Barrels Ale House (01289 308013), in Berwick-upon-Tweed, hosts a selection of local cask ales and live music but is a 20-minute drive away. While you're in town, check out the farmers' market in the Maltings (01289 330999) on the last Sunday of every month. Or do as the monks did and sup some Lindisfarne Mead at St Aidan's Winery (01289 389230; www.lindisfarne-mead.co.uk). There's oysters aplenty, too, on Holy Island (01668 213870; www.lindisfarneoysters.co.uk).

🏕️ Open mid February through to the end of December.

🏕️ Wigwams cost £15 to £20 per adult per night and children £9 to £10, depending on the season. Big yurts cost £85 for 6 people (sleeps up to 8), and small ones £65 for 4 people (sleeps up to 6); extra guests cost £10 per night.

Sounding like some weird kind of experiment with a cockerel and a ready meal, Pot-a-Doodle Do also looks a bit whacky. Imagine, if you will, a small collection of wooden wigwams sitting on the Northumberland coast (there are some yurts now, too); it looks like a geographically misplaced scene from a Western. Now, if you're up for some Cowboys and Indians, let's get rolling, rolling, rolling…

Each of the 20 wigwams sleeps up to five people and is powered by an electric hook-up, providing heat, light, and a small fridge. And when the North Sea decides to teach the land who's boss, you'll be thankful you're under something super-sturdy.

The three yurts are cosy with wood-burners, wooden floors, and futons. Throw in some candlelight and a clear skylight for indoor stargazing, and you're set for some enchanting evenings. The site is family focussed, with activities galore in its creative art centre and cross-country quad-biking for a range of ages.

Nearby tidal Holy Island holds many attractions, but make sure you check the tide times in advance to save yourself – and your car – from a dip in the sea. Lindisfarne Castle, built by the monastic demolition expert Henry VIII, who pillaged stone from the now skeletal local priory, sits atop a volcanic mound at the island's end and looks imperiously out to sea.

You, too, can venture seawards for some ornithologist action on the Farne Islands – one of the UK's top sea-bird sanctuaries, colonised by thousands of puffins, divebomber terns, and guillemots. It's probably a good idea to wear some kind of hat for protection – but preferably not of the cowboy variety.

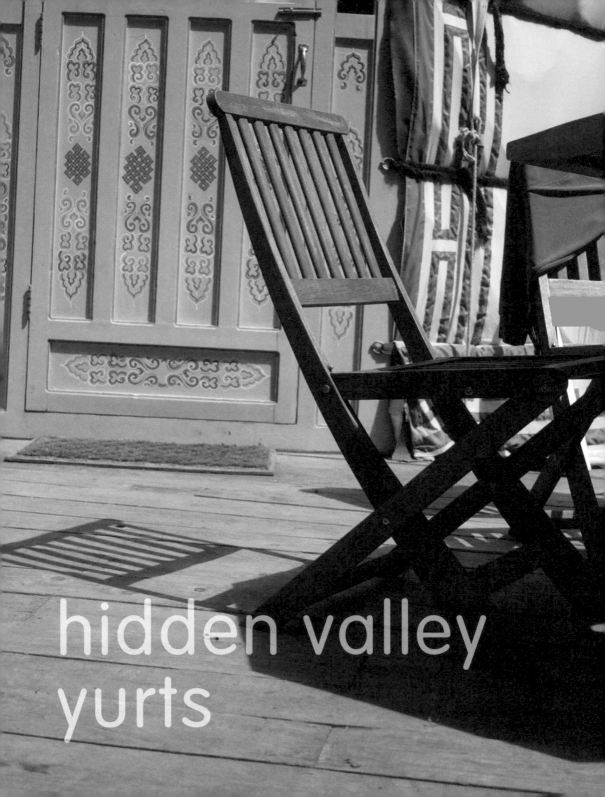

hidden valley
yurts

Hidden Valley Yurts are exactly that. Invisible to, and inaccessible from, the outside world, these homely canvas abodes freckle the green face of a picturesque Monmouthshire valley overlooking a gurgling stream and shielded by trees… But if they're inaccessible, how do you get there? Good question – and one that has a really fun answer.

Guests arrive innocuously enough by car, which is then abandoned in the car park – often for the entirety of their stay. They then present themselves at the farmhouse to be warmly greeted by Amanda or Peter, who chauffeur them to their yurt. But this is no ordinary service, as the vehicle in question is an all-terrain buggy, without doors, windscreen, or roof, for that matter.

There are two seats up front and at the back the Ute-style flat-bed trailer is handy for luggage and an extra body or two. As it bounces along the track and down the near-vertical field, one of the two farm dogs bounding alongside, it becomes clear why this type of transport is the only wheel way to get to the yurts. It chugs effortlessly along another stony track, across a ford and a puddle or two, before arriving at the yurts, which feel miles from anywhere in this hidden valley.

There are six yurts altogether, stretching higgledy-piggledy along the field; three of

them sleeping five people and the other three accommodating up to seven. The yurts' felt roofs and wall linings are ultra thick and made from pure sheep's wool. Step through one of the brightly coloured doors of these innovative homes to find it lovingly bedecked with beds, rugs, and wall-hangings, and equipped with a wood-burning stove and copper kettle, with a bag of kindling for fuel. And each yurt has a built-in BBQ and solar fairy lights.

The comfortable feel of each yurt entreats you to curl up and unwind, having spent the

day wandering around the cool woodland, flower-peppered meadows, and fields belonging to the farm's 80 acres. You may even spot one of Amanda's eco-friendly 'pretty lawnmowers' on your travels. No, these aren't machines painted pink, but doe-eyed, woolly alpacas that will happily keep any lawn from getting out of hand.

A designated Area of Outstanding Natural Beauty, this corner of Wales, often overlooked in favour of better-known Pembrokeshire and Snowdonia, has been blessed by Mother Nature and wildlife abounds here. Hidden Valley is home to many species of butterfly, including the über-rare Dingy Skipper (its name does this little critter's pretty, patterned wings a disservice) as well as bees, spiders, and bats, so be sure to pack your bug boxes and spotters' guides to do the Bill Oddie thing.

A large wooden communal kitchen and bathroom area boasts the kind of veranda that would make *Gone-With-The-Wind*-type southerners jealous, and provides just the spot for whiling away evenings in a hammock. Below the veranda, there's a boules pitch, campfire area, wood-burning pizza oven, and help-yourself herb garden, along with a large safari tent for outdoor eating; just some of the thoughtful touches that make this place one of those extra-special camping experiences.

## Hidden Valley Yurts

Lower Glyn Farm, Llanishen, Chepstow,
Monmouthshire, NP16 6QU
www.hiddenvalleyyurts.co.uk

🐌 Immaculate and sustainable yurt camping.
Choose from 6 yurts, one of which has its own
compost loo and tented kitchen. There's a large
kitchen and communal bathroom 'block' on
wooden decking, with picnic tables and hammock
overlooking the valley. The kitchen has all you need
and the bathroom has 2 showers and 2 loos. All
water comes from a local spring and is flushed away
on to a reed bed. There's another kitchen area and
rustic compost loos not far off, and a small kitchen
between the first 2 yurts. The main kitchen has a
breadmaker and built-in BBQ.

🐌 It's easy to while away the hours in Monmouth,
a pretty little town with nice shops and a couple of
decent pubs. Tintern (www.tintern.org.uk) is fairly
near, with its majestic abbey ruins made famous by
Turner's painting and Wordsworth's poem.

🐌 Just a mile away, in Llanishen, (though it's uphill
all the way) is the Carpenter's Arms (01600 860812;
www.carpentersarmsllanishen.co.uk). But you're
spoiled for choice in this area for good food: there's
the Raglan Arms (01291 690800; www.
theraglanarms.co.uk) in Llandenny, the Hardwick
(01873 854220; www.thehardwick.co.uk) in
Abergavenny, the award-winning Foxhunter (01873
881101; www.thefoxhunter.com) in Nantyderry,
and the Michelin-starred Crown at Whitebrook
(01600 860254; www.crownatwhitebrook.co.uk) –
all of which lie within half-an-hour's drive.

🐌 Open early April to late September.

🐌 A weekend break of 3 nights, midweek break of
4 nights, or a combination to make up a week's stay
in a yurt costs from £225 to £440, depending on
how long you're staying.

mandinam

There's an old saying at Mandinam: 'If you're not bothered, then I don't give a damn.' You could be forgiven for thinking that Marcus, the owner, is somewhat apathetic. However, his motto simply means as long as his guests don't have a worry, then neither does he. And you're given free reign to do whatever you want within these 450 acres of idyllic Welsh farmland, in the middle of nowhere.

Marcus makes for an interesting and engaging host, happy to chat about anything from the woes of today's farming industry to the animals he tends on his land. And you'll soon notice that he has put just as much care and attention into his shepherd's hut and gypsy caravan as he has into the entire farm.

If it's privacy you're after, then either of these wooden huts offers it in droves, as well as a view destined to hurt your eyes if you stare at it too much: gaping-wide, open rolling hills. It really is the place to lose inhibitions and get stuck into unadulterated chilling.

Once you snap out of your scenic trance, just step inside your chosen abode and prepare to coo at how dainty and cosy it is. Beautifully furnished, every inch of both huts exudes the love that has been put into them, from the mini-kitchen with butler sink to the traditional wood-burning stove. Equipped with everything that the camper's heart could desire, they even come complete with fresh lavender to aid a peaceful night's slumber. The only things you'll need to concern yourself with are when to light the BBQ and what time to climb into the hot tub, which sits next to the gypsy caravan. Yes, a hot tub – on a hill – with an impressive sea of stunning farmland for a view, and the jealous stars as an audience.

Welsh legend has it that 'Mandinam' means 'a place without blemish' or 'untouched holy place', and after one night's stay here, you'll see just how fitting these descriptions are.

## Mandinam

Llangadog, Carmarthenshire, SA19 9LA
www.mandinam.co.uk

 Both the gypsy caravan and shepherd's hut come with kitchenettes, a twin gas-stove, a wood-burner, double bed with luxurious bedding, kitchenware, BBQ, and separate en suite bathroom; campfires are allowed too. Gas-powered shower in the gypsy caravan, log-burning shower in the shepherd's hut. The latter also has a separate compost toilet. Both have solar-powered lighting and outdoor seating areas, and the gypsy hut comes with its own outdoor hot tub. You can charge mobiles and batteries in Marcus' home.

The 450 acres of Mandinam provide plenty of walking, birdwatching, fishing, and bat-spotting opportunities. However, if you venture 12 miles further you'll find the National Botanic Garden of Wales (01558 668768; www.gardenofwales.org.uk) and a selection of Welsh castles, including Carreg Cennen (www.castlewales.com).

For decent pub grub, the Red Lion (01550 777357; www.redlioncoachinginn.co.uk) ticks all the right boxes and is only a short walk into Llangadog village. But for some real Carmarthenshire finesse, book a table at Y Polyn (01267 290000; www. ypolynrestaurant.co.uk) in Capel Dewi.

Open all year.

Both shepherd's hut and gypsy caravan are £70 per night, with a minimum stay of 2 nights.

larkhill tipis

In the stillness of the Teifi Valley, not far from the bubbling Bargoed stream, can be found the most perfect countryside retreat. And even though it's an entirely artificial invention, from the creative brains and dextrous hands of Tony and Fran Wintle, it feels like the most natural place on earth.

Larkhill used to be just a simple family home surrounded by open farmland. But Fran and Tony had a plan – to turn this place into a peaceful woodland hideaway, far from modern life's stresses and strains. They began planting trees – oak, beech, ash, and field maple; in total, 60 different species now thrive in what is a remarkable transformation. At intervals, throughout the fledgling woodland, they levelled off terraces and began constructing tipis and yurts in the small clearings, in order to share this quiet corner with guests.

Tony designed and built a hexagonal log cabin, in keeping with the wood-rich environment, to serve as a kitchen and dining room. Through the centre of the land they planted an avenue of laburnum trees, which flower gloriously every spring in a riot of yellow. At the end of this dazzling walkway, a curious seven-ringed maze is scorched into the earth and, on occasion, it's lit, to become a spectacular labyrinth of fire. A wild flower meadow occupies the unforested areas of the

20 acres, and, in addition, there are a number of quiet corners and wooded glades hidden around the place – ideal for those who like meditation, contemplation, and relaxation.

In essence, Fran and Tony have restored a small slice of ancient Welsh woodland to its former charming and mystical glory. This is a fantastic example of a low-impact, sustainable tourism initiative, as well as being a great way to utilise redundant farmland.

The care and attention that has been lavished on this place is obvious at every turn.

Wooden benches have been hand-crafted and positioned for maximum view-enjoyment. Paving stones have been individually designed, with patterns inspired by nature. Even the showers and electricity at Larkhill are powered by solar panels and wind turbines.

There are five different nomadic camping experiences at Larkhill, each equipped with comfortable beds, a box full of warm blankets, and a central fire or wood-burning stove. The most luxurious option is the spacious Alachigh: an Iranian nomadic tent, that's a cross between a yurt and a tipi; it even has a breakfast bar with jaw-dropping views of the stunning Welsh landscape. The two yurt-like dwellings (well, one is actually a ger and the other an oba) are warm, weatherproof, and sleep four comfortably. And when the sun shines, you'll wonder at the ever-changing leaf shadows dancing on your rooftop, since each abode sits in sylvan surroundings. Last but not least there's the tipi, which has a central chimenea to funnel smoke out of the top.

There are plenty of attractions around here, but rushing around isn't really the point of a holiday at Larkhill. It's about chilling out in a wonderfully peaceful valley, sitting around a campfire, enjoying the countryside vistas, and listening to the larks of Larkhill calling softly. Sheer bliss. With extra shhh.

## Larkhill Tipis

Cwmduad, Carmarthenshire, SA33 6AT
www.larkhilltipis.co.uk

There are 5 different canvas abodes to choose from: an Iranian tribal tent (sleeps 6), and a yurt, a ger, a tipi, and a lavvu (Scandinavian dwelling), all of which sleep 4. Beds, cushions, pillows, and extra blankets are included; bring your own sleeping bag, food, towel, and torch. Pots, pans, crockery, cutlery, and a cool box are all supplied; you can cook on an open fire, the BBQ, or on gas hobs. There's also a cooker in the log cabin, along with a sink for washing up and low-voltage power for charging things. Two hot showers are available in another log cabin; you can choose between a surprisingly posh, neutral-smelling compost toilet or a conventional flusher. There's also a small children's play area to keep youngsters entertained on site.

Try your hand at weaving at the free National Wool Museum (01559 370929; see www.museumwales.ac.uk) in Llandysul. They also have leaflets at Larkhill about the local taste trail (www.walesthetruetaste.co.uk), the splendid National Botanic Garden (01558 668768; www.gardenofwales.org.uk), and local kayaking.

For food, the Afon Duad Inn (01267 281357; www.afonduad.com), 3 miles away in Cwmduad, offers a good vegetarian menu and a selection of sturdy Welsh meat dishes. Further afield is the bright-yellow John-y-Gwas tavern (01559 370469), which offers good grub in a cosy bar.

The ger, yurt, and Iranian tent are open all year. The tipi and lavvu are available April to October.

Prices start from £60 a night for a tipi or lavvu, going up to £600 for a week in the Iranian tent.

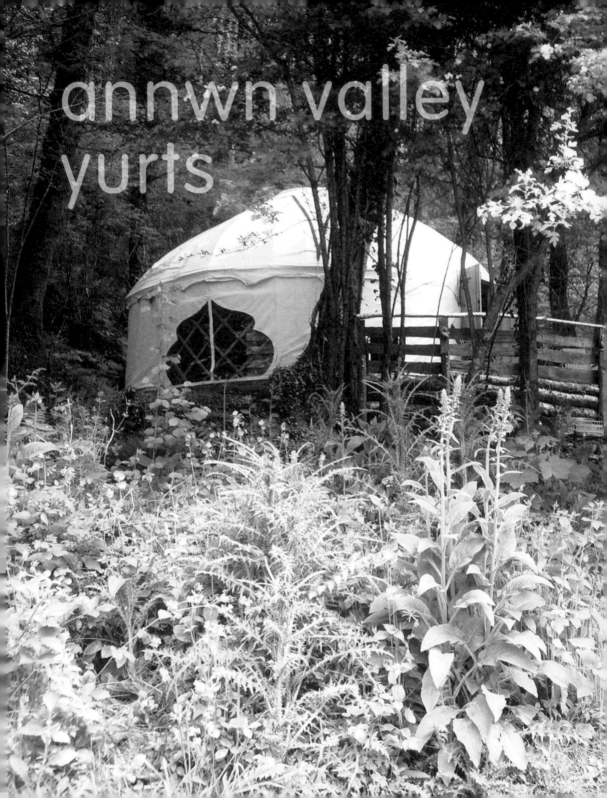

Welcome to Annwn – a rapturous world of enchantment, where illness is non-existent and food is forever bountiful… Those who are up to date with their Welsh mythology will know that we're actually referring to the Welsh Otherworld, to which, to this day, there are supposed gateways scattered across Wales. Cych Valley, where Annwn Valley Yurts rests, happens to be one of them.

Driving along Carmarthenshire's twists and turns, you'll most likely drive straight past Annwn Valley. But, perhaps by the power of the fairies (or satnav), you'll undoubtedly turn around and drive straight to Carmen's door.

And what hosts Carmen and her sidekick – Rani the dog – are. Known by everyone throughout the Cych Valley, Carmen is half the reason to come and stay at Annwn. She manages to take the make-yourself-at-home ethos to new heights of generosity as she shows you around her solar-powered, fairy-lit wonderland. And, in case you were wondering, Carmen's yurts make up the other half of the reason to stay here.

The words 'decadent', 'rich', and 'warm' fail to do justice to the ambience of an Annwn Valley yurt, where you'll instantly feel like the proverbial cat that got the cream among the red velvet, sheepskin rugs, gold and crimson embroidery, and glowing candle lanterns. The stunning detail of the yurts runs all the way from the mystifying pattern in the antique rugs, up along the hand-crafted oak trellis, and finishes at your very own see-through portal to the stars, at the centre of the roof.

Adding to the site's overall mystique and Otherworldliness are all the little touches Carmen has put into the place to give it her unique stamp. From the (fittingly) Fairy Liquid, to the cafetière, wind-up torches, and abundance of chopped firewood, you will be left wanting for nothing.

It is tough, but do drag yourself out of your Annwn yurt-world, and explore the wooded valley on your yurtstep. Wander alongside a stream, resplendent with resilient salmon, towards ancient woodlands and admire Mother Nature doing what she does best.

If your stay here leaves you welling up at the thought of leaving, then why not take a piece of Annwn home? Carmen is a sculptress extraordinaire; check out her controversial takes on love hearts… They're bound to elicit giggles before you depart this Otherworld.

## Annwn Valley Yurts

Pont Cych Mill, Cwm Cych, Newcastle Emlyn,
Carmarthenshire, SA38 9RR
www.annwnvalley.co.uk

🫖 Both the yurts (each sleeping up to 5) are
nothing short of visual masterpieces, complete
with antique rugs, sheepskins, floor cushions, tables,
storage, and soft lighting (candles and lanterns).
Each comes with 1 double and 3 single futons;
bedding (£10) and extra futons are available on
request. You have an internal and external kitchen
area to choose from too; the internal one comprises
a wood-burning stove, a small kitchen area with a
gas cooker, plus crockery (every type possible), and
utensils. Outside you have a BBQ (with firelighters),
picnic table, and bundles of free firewood. There's
fresh running water, a very modern and clean
compost toilet, and your own recycling and
washing-up area (with Fairy Liquid and a sponge).
One main shower block with a free warm shower,
toilet, and fridge-freezer. Carmen will gladly let
you use her kitchen for cooking, plus sockets for
charging. There's a beautiful river nearby and lush
flowers and faeries to look out for.

🫖 Don your walking boots and explore the magical
Cych Valley woodlands right on your doorstep. Flit
along with the butterflies at the Butterfly Farm in
Aberystwyth (01970 880928; www.magicoflife.org);
or drive down to the Cardigan coast – only 10 miles
away – for dolphin sightings and stunning views.

🫖 The Nags Head (01239 841200) pub in Abercych
is only a short walk away and serves a mean lamb
shank plus a wide selection of ales. Newcastle Emlyn
also offers a host of superb restaurants.

🫖 Open for weekly bookings in August only, so
book well in advance.

🫖 Yurts cost £650 per week.

The track leading up to Flimstone Farm can only be described as magical – numerous tree tunnels and twisted, gnarled branches accompany you along the way; the stuff of fairy tales in preparation for the enchanting yurt holiday that awaits.

This farm is home to just one yurt – and we're talking the real Mongolian deal – silk-lined, beautifully hand-painted, and, by jingo, it's massive. Depending on how well you know your yurt-fellows (or maybe how well you want to know them by the end of the holiday), it can sleep up to a cosy six people in a double bed and four single futons. And bang in the middle of the yurt is a pot-bellied stove; while there's a tripod BBQ for cooking outside.

The yurt's biggest fan is resident cat (and camping enthusiast) Humbug. He oversees the annual erection of the structure and just hates to see it being taken down again each winter. He'll often pop down, from time to time, to see if any new campers have arrived.

Maybe the best thing about this yurt holiday is the flexibility it offers. You can stay put in your flower meadow and use the cold spring-water and BBQ to cook with, for a more rustic glamping experience. Or else, feel at liberty to dash into the farmhouse for a steaming hot shower and use of the fully equipped kitchen. The choice is yours.

Humbug thinks the yurt is the best idea owner Val's ever had, and, with the luxurious facilities just a pounce away and a games room in the pipeline, we're inclined to agree.

## Flimstone Farm

Robeston Wathen, Narberth, Pembrokeshire, SA67 8EY
www.flimstonefarmholidays.co.uk

There's just 1 yurt, but it's huge. You'll find a fully equipped bathroom and kitchen in the farmhouse, a short walk away. Inside, there's a gas hob and a wood-burning stove. Campfires are allowed in fire pits; logs and your first bag of charcoal are included.

The ancient coastal town of Tenby is just a short drive away, as are all kinds of watery activities, dotted along the nearby Pembrokeshire coast. And wildlife enthusiasts will flock to Skomer Island to see its spectacular array of bird life as well as wild flower meadows and impressive coastline. You'll find a large selection of brochures in the yurt if you're short of inspiration.

The Bridge Dining Room & Lounge Bar (01834 860541; www.thebridgediningroom.co.uk), on the Narberth Road, is neither pub nor restaurant, but the food is really very good; ask to eat in the lounge bar for a more relaxed dining experience. The market town of Narberth is a 5-minute drive away, where you will find the über-deli Ultracomida (01834 861491; www.ultracomida.co.uk) as well as plenty of cafés and restaurants.

Open from early April to the end of October.

A week in a yurt costs £390 to £520, or £190 to £240 for a 3-night break, depending on the season.

mill haven
place

If Cath Kidston imagined herself a yurt camp, it would look something like Mill Haven Place – all floral bunting, spotty tablecloths, and enamelware, and – oh my – it is pretty.

Owners Josie Coggins and Matt Oliver are ruthlessly devoted to making this site truly unforgettable. Having opened the site only in 2009, after more than six years of building and renovating their own home and barn, Josie and Matt have already established a beautiful, welcoming community of four picture-perfect yurts. They've also planted a swathe of 1,500 new trees, which, when mature, will transform the site into a miniature woodland.

Three generations of Josie's family live on the site, and the place definitely has a warm feel of 'family' about it. Unlike other yurt sites, where individual units are secluded or set among woodland, here at Mill Haven Place they are clustered around the young copse and are close enough to create a camp community.

The yurts sit atop their very own deck, which, aside from being a lovely place to sit and sip your sundowner, helps enormously with the general cosiness of the yurts. The structures themselves can sleep four – with a double and two singles. The doubles being beautiful cast-iron beds complete with snuggly Welsh blankets. And yes, more bunting. One of the best things about the yurts is their smell – the delicate tinge of woodsmoke from the tiny stoves that sit within each one.

You get the impression that Matt could more or less turn his hand to anything: from bushcraft sessions at the site, where he'll show you how to light the perfect campfire, to preparing and cooking the mackerel you've caught that very day, while out sea-kayaking.

Mill Haven Place seems like the happiest, most welcoming yurt site you can imagine. And we think you and Cath would agree, it takes a lot more than bunting to achieve that.

## Mill Haven Place

Middle Broadmoor, Talbenny, Haverfordwest,
Pembrokeshire, SA62 3XD
www.millhavenplace.co.uk

🐾 Four yurts, 5 pitches for camping. Four toilets
(2 compost), 3 showers, 2 washing-up sinks.
Drinking water is from a bore hole. Campfires are
allowed and your first trug of logs is free, then £4
after that. BBQs are also provided. Each yurt has its
own camp kitchen with gas hob, cool box, and all
the cooking paraphernalia you could ever want.
There are some charming touches: solar-powered
fairy lights, paper lanterns, wooden-bench seating,
brightly coloured table cloths, and, yes, more
bunting. Meanwhile, 2 compost loos and a
salubrious decked shower/wet-room comprise the
site's ablutions, plus fantastic recycling facilities.

🐾 Mill Haven Beach is 1 mile away down a quiet
farm track. The marine reserve of Skomer Island can
be seen from the site — there are puffins to be
spotted and seals in mid July. TYF Adventure (01437
721611; www.tyf.com) in St David's offers kayaking,
coasteering, rock-climbing, surfing, and fishing.

🐾 In Little Haven, the Swan Inn (01437 781880;
www.theswanlittlehaven.co.uk) serves real ale and
very fresh seafood. Matt and Josie produce some
salads and seasonal veg on the farm. Check out
Pembrokeshire Produce Direct (01437 563035;
www.pembrokeshireproducedirect.org.uk) for
fresh, local produce that can be delivered to the
site. There are farmers' markets every other Friday
in Haverfordwest (01437 776168; www.
pembrokeshirefarmersmarkets.co.uk). The Londis
in Broad Haven also sells seasonal veg boxes.

🐾 Open from late April to late September.

🐾 Weekly prices for a yurt are £390 to £550
(depending on the season). You can hire a yurt
for a weekend only in low season (£160).

# pembrokeshire tipis

Dust off your headdress and polish your
moccasins, for if you go down to Simpson
Cross today, you're sure of a wig(wam)
surprise. A pasture reserved for grazing horses
in the winter months is transformed into
a vision from the prairies of the Wild West
come summer, with the addition of three
rather magnificent tipis.

Drive through a field speckled with tents,
campervans, and the occasional small caravan,
to emerge into a second field. This expanse
of lush meadow is further from the road and
shielded from view by a hotchpotch hedge
of gorse, bramble, and bracken. A carefully
mown track leads you to your tipi, as the
flowery field tumbles gently down into a
valley. In the early morning, it's so full of
swirling mists it looks like an ocean
stretching out before you.

The tipis march majestically down the
hill, keeping a civilised distance from one
another, their doorways facing shyly into the
well-established hedgerow, sheltered from
the wind and from view. Ready and waiting
for your arrival, each tipi is labelled with a
tag on the door of its lovingly hand-crafted
kitchen structure, giving the proceedings an
almost treasure-hunt feel.

Once you're inside, you'll find everything
you could possibly need for knocking up

some serious culinary creations, and outside it's topped off with a tufty green roof.

Des, the site's owner, has also provided an enchantingly eclectic bookshelf, with tomes on anything from the Bauhaus to the art of good pig-keeping. The shelf itself is a structural marvel, held up by a complex rope suspension system. It's a reflection of how this place works – everything is here, everything has been considered, but guests aren't mollycoddled. This is not the glossy, Sunday-supplement idea of glamping; it's much better: it's basic enough to give you that heady sense of adventure, but there's enough kit to make it super-comfy and fuss free.

Outside the tipis, you'll find a stone-encircled fire pit and a rustic but effective cast-iron BBQ, replete with everything you might need in order to make fire – perfect for the armchair-Bear Grylls among us. So, once you've sparked the kindling and managed to coax the fire into life, wrap yourself in the cosy woven blankets, lie back, and watch the smoke rising from your campfire, carrying with it all your thoughts and dreams up to the powerful spirits in the starlit Pembrokeshire sky.

Now, Des doesn't really like the idea of signs; he's a big believer in the common sense of the camper. And anyway, who wants to be

told what to do on holiday? You just have to trust that Des and his wife Jane have quietly thought of everything, and then added a little bit more. Enjoy the thrill of discovering it all for yourself without the 'help' of a ringbound welcome pack. In Des' own words, if he were to put up a sign, it would probably say something along the lines of 'Don't throw stones at this sign'. Having said that, you shouldn't be surprised to find him in the lane's hedge on your arrival, surreptitiously adding a feathered headdress to the rider on the horse sign – it's a thankless task, though, as he's yet to find a sufficiently weatherproof pen.

## Pembrokeshire Tipis

Simpson Cross, Pembrokeshire, SA62 6ET
www.pembrokeshiretipis.co.uk

🏕️ The 3 tipis (sleep 4: 1 double futon and 2 singles) share a huge field. Each has its own picnic bench, BBQ, fire pit, and kitchen shack, complete with 2-ring gas hob, grill, running water, and all cooking and eating equipment. Campfires are allowed in fire pits and enough fuel is provided for your first night. After that, logs and charcoal can be bought from Des. There is a solar-heated shower attached to the side of each shack, but you can also use a small facilities block in the camping field.

🏕️ The site is just a tomahawk's throw (not that this is recommended) away from Nolton Stables (01437 710360; www.noltonstables.com), which offers breathtaking beach rides up to Druidstone Haven and caters for all abilities. A trip to Folly Farm (01834 812731; www.folly-farm.co.uk) near Kilgetty is an enchanting day out for younger children, with adventure playgrounds, farm animals, and a zoo housing the only giraffe in Wales. But, of course, the main attraction in these parts is the Coastal National Park and its beaches and bays.

🏕️ See if you can spot a dolphin while you sip a pint on the terrace at the quirky Druidstone Hotel (01437 781221; www.druidstone.co.uk). If the gales are a-blowing, retreat to its walled garden and play chess with pieces made of hand-painted pebbles. Get some local produce at the farmers' market in Haverfordwest (www.pembrokeshirefarmersmarkets. co.uk) every other Friday, or pop to the farm down the road from the campsite for super-fresh eggs.

🏕️ Open from Easter to late September/early October (weather dependent).

🏕️ Each tipi costs £50 to £70 per night, depending on the season and length of stay.

A step, a leap, and an icy plunge into the blue lagoon at an old slate quarry make the splashing finale to coasteering, at its Pembrokeshire birthplace. An alternative way of exploring the coastline, coasteering involves using bare hands and trainered toes to scrabble along rocky cliffs, interspersed with jumps into the waves from varying heights. Not one for the fainthearted!

Coasteering is one of many endorphin-inducing activities offered by the fforest outdoor team, as part of their 'active relaxation' philosophy; a clever concept that helps clear the mind through learning new skills and the physical demands of a tough day's play. And it really works. Canoeing down the serene River Teifi, horse-riding, cycling, bushcraft courses, and sealife-spotting off Cardigan Island are just some of fforest's sure-fire ways to de-clutter minds and reacquaint cheeks with fresh air.

fforest outdoor is the brainchild of James and Sîan, who also own fforest at Cilgerran, a slice of the tastiest rural pie, which they thankfully saw fit to share. Sitting in a peaceful pocket of Ceredigion countryside, this family-run former farm is only a couple of miles' trundle upriver from colourful Cardigan, where the activities team is based. It's the perfect place to unwind and feel soothed by all the good countryside sounds – birdsong, chirping crickets, and breeze-kissed boughs – whether you've spent the day cliff-scrambling, shopping, walking, or just want to put distance between yourself and your normal routine.

Fascinated by what makes a dwelling 'home' rather than simply a place to sleep, James toyed with the idea of installing eco-lodges, before settling on stylish canvas accommodation in the shape of nomad tunnel tents, bell tents, threepis (tipis), and grand domes all the way from America. And an old barn has been converted into four croglofts – maisonette lodges, each with its own beds, sofa, and bathroom.

The dwellings have been dotted around the hilly farmland in fields and among the trees.

At night, muted tangerine glows from lanterns lead you down to the lodge, which is the communal hub of the place before folk head to the fire pits to gaze at hypnotic flames over a tasty local beverage from the onsite 'pub'. Adjoining the pub is a makeshift cinema, with straw stacks providing rural pews for guests to perch on while they enjoy weekly film nights.

Every possible need has been considered: each nomad tunnel tent, tipi, and dome has its own 'kitchen' and sits on sturdy wooden decking, from which you can admire picture-postcard views of fields in green and gold, sprinkled with languid deer. The decking eradicates any worries about bumpy surfaces, damp, and mud that can't help but creep into a tent pitched on the ground. There's wi-fi for those who can't go without and, for a touch of serious pampering, a sauna (which came flat-packed from Sweden – where else?) is tucked among the trees.

In terms of a sanctuary, celeb 'rehab' haunt the Priory has got nothing on fforest. The trowel-loads of care and pride that James and Sîan have lavished on the place will no doubt transform your breathing into long, contented sighs soon after you arrive.

This is not just camping; this is fforest camping – a relaxed and comforting tonic to everyday life that easily slips into your being.

## fforest

fforest farm, Cilgerran, Ceredigion, SA43 2TB,
www.coldatnight.co.uk

The nomad tents, bell tents, threepis, and domes sleep between 4 and 6 people. Each sits on wooden decking, which acts as a veranda, too, where you'll find a large bean-bag and comfy chairs, as well as a kitchen with cool boxes, water cooler, crockery, gas hobs, and a kettle. Inside the bell tents, threepis, and domes you'll find an indoor stove with wood, kindling, and matches to help keep you snug at night. The ablutional facilities are immaculate. A large wooden block in the threepi and bell tent field has 4 hot showers (and basins in the cubicles), 4 loos, 4 sinks with Ecover soap, and 2 washing-up sinks. The communal lodge serves breakfast daily and is open in the evenings. On Friday and Monday evenings delicious dinners are served to those who fancy it, which is a nice way to meet fellow campers.

Take your pick from wet activities such as kayaking or coasteering with the fforest outdoor team, or head into Cardigan for a mosey around the shops. Otherwise stay put and head for the sauna; a rota for its use can be found in the lodge.

Be sure to check out the wonderful onsite 'pub' in a rustic old farm building next to the cabin. It has a toasty log fire and is lit by candle 'chandeliers', which give the place an ethereal, romantic glow. The slightly smoky atmosphere and hotchpotch seating help create a really cosy feel. Organic wines and local beer and ciders are sold (added to your tab).

Open April to October; the croglofts are also available in the winter months.

It's best to check the website for prices, which range from £230 for a midweek stay in a nomad tent in April to £1,040 for a week's stay in a crogloft during the summer holidays. Prices are based on B&B for 2 people. Additional adults cost £10 per night, £7 per additional child, and dogs £4 per night.

under the
thatch

Camping can be wildly romantic. Picture the scene: two people sheltering from the elements, cooking on a simple fire, enjoying secluded countryside together. And thanks to Under the Thatch, this heady mixture has been elevated to another level entirely.

Under the Thatch specialises in finding derelict or disused Welsh buildings of architectural significance, restoring them to their former glory, and setting them up for holiday lets. The idea is to get the buildings contributing to the rural economy, rather than to its decline. The name originates from their first few projects, for which age-old cottages were restored and rethatched in traditional wheat straw, but they've since branched out to other, more unusual, accommodations, one of them being a beautiful Romany caravan.

The caravan – or vardo, to use its correct name – was originally built in 1924 by highly reputable wagon builders Wood Bros and, after years of heavy use and more years sitting in various hay barns doing nothing, was acquired by the gang at Under the Thatch in 2004. They set about restoring it, staying true to the original Romany design and colour scheme. The result is a magnificently authentic holiday time capsule. The brightly painted wood accentuates the heroic craftsmanship, the bow-top roof curves

impossibly – like a bubble ready to burst – and the tiny half-and-half doors need only a large-busted Romany mother leaning out to make them any more authentic.

The cosy interior is similarly themed. A sturdy wooden double bed is built across the back of the caravan, with just enough space for a traditional pot-belly stove and some wooden cupboards in which to stash your stuff. A few steps from the caravan, a rustic cabin is on hand to provide extra storage, as well as a shower, hand basin, toilet, and a full

range of kitchen accoutrements including fridge and oven. There's even a small sitting area with a CD player, a bit like an extra chill-out room in case the caravan gets too claustrophobic for comfort, or you feel like taking a quick break from your other half.

Both the caravan and the cabin are located in their own small meadow, which follows the banks of the River Ceri, a clean, shallow river perfect for splashing around in of a hot summer afternoon. You might even spot brown trout and otters darting around the waters. From the steps of the caravan, all that can be seen in any direction is green countryside, which adds to the secluded and oh-so-romantic experience.

It's a short drive to the beaches of Tresaith, Llangrannog, and Penbryn, and a slightly longer one to the pretty Georgian harbour town of Aberaeron, with its colour-washed houses and old-time pubs; worth the trip if you feel like a little outing. Since the Romany caravan has become so popular, Under the Thatch have restored more cosy vardos, a shepherd's hut, and a couple of circus-showman's wagons, any of which are irresistible for all those who fancy a romantic break for two. After all, in a snug wooden room only a few feet wide you won't need an excuse to get cosy with each other.

## Under the Thatch

Romany Caravan, Felin Brithdir, Rhydlewis, Llandysul,
Ceredigion, SA44 5SN
www.underthethatch.co.uk

🐾 A vardo for 2 in its own meadow. Adjacent to the
little caravan is a wooden shack set up like a
self-catering cabin, with everything you could need,
including a hot shower, fully equipped kitchen, and a
covered veranda. Fuel is provided for the caravan
stove on arrival and an electric blanket is available if
it gets a bit nippy. Bedding is provided.

🐾 Apart from exploring the Ceredigion coast or
wandering around Aberaeron, the biggest attraction
is the Llanerchaeron country estate (01545 570200;
see www.nationaltrust.org.uk), now in the hands of
the National Trust. This 18th-century Welsh gentry
holding was designed and built by John Nash. The
house has already been restored, but just like the
mission of the Under the Thatch team, the idea is
for the estate to contribute to the local economy
so it's become a self-sustaining organic farm.

🐾 The Harbourmaster Hotel (01545 570755;
www.harbour-master.com), right on the harbour in
Aberaeron, is worth the half-hour drive. It's a
foodie's delight, with lobster, crab, and fish fresh
from Cardigan Bay; local lamb and venison; and
Welsh Black beef. Bread is baked on the premises.
A bar menu is available as well as the restaurant's
(mains £12–£22). A closer option is the Ship Inn at
Tresaith (01239 811816; www.shiptresaith.co.uk).

🐾 Open all year.

🐾 From £202 to £457 for a short stay and from
£336 to £610 for a week, depending on the season.
Dogs are welcome to accompany guests.

the yurt farm

Yurts. Suddenly they're everywhere. Just a few short years ago they were a rare breed in the Welsh countryside, an exotic novelty. 'Look — there's a yurt! Wow, never seen one of those before.' But then, following the success of pioneers like Larkhill (p140), Wales has been inundated with these rotund little pods. If you'd lived in Wales pre-yurt, had been away for some years, and were now returning home by helicopter, you might well assume (as you surveyed the numerous round tents placed across the countryside like white draughts on a checkerboard) that Wales had been invaded in your absence by nomadic tribes from the Central Asian steppe. That's a ridiculous notion, of course, because a) virtually no-one in Wales travels around in a helicopter, except maybe Charlotte Church, and b) this invasion is one of UK-ation glampers, not nomadic tribes looking for more fertile terrain.

But one thing that the glamping brigade need note is that not all yurts are equal. While many outfits are reputable and well run, there are also those yurts propped up in fields/back gardens operated by charlatans who just want to make a quick buck. You have been warned.

Thankfully, at the Yurt Farm, Thea and Laurie know what they're doing. And they do it very well. This place hasn't been thrown together, it's been thought through, planned out, then nurtured and loved into existence. Breathing new life into a forgotten corner of a large organic farm in Ceredigion, this collection of five yurts is less about the accommodation itself and more about fully immersing yourself in this off-beat, off-grid, off-the-beaten-track hideaway.

A spacious hay meadow gives each yurt as much room as some other campsites might give 30 tents. The yurts are warm and cosy, not to mention impeccably well maintained. The location is perfect: ridiculously remote

and enveloped in the sort of rich, green countryside for which Wales is famous. And the love is evident everywhere: a welcome basket of tasty veg for guests, unique four-poster beds fashioned out of trees, and wheelbarrows on hand for transporting your gear (vehicles are not allowed on site).

The guys here also deserve brownie points for making this place as environmentally sensitive as possible. With herb-box fridges, reed-bed drainage, comfy hand-built compost loos, and the careful use of locally sourced and reclaimed building materials, this canvas commune is truly low impact. Solar panels keep the showers warm while a wind turbine provides enough power to charge torches, but that's it for modern madness.

Most of your time will be spent outdoors, with the striking Cambrian mountains as your backdrop. There are 150 acres to be discovered, criss-crossed by a network of farm trails; children are free to explore, make dens, hide in the long grass, play in the sand, hang off rope swings, collect eggs, be licked by cows, and gorge themselves on blackcurrants and gooseberries from the yurt meadow.

It might have been the quirky yurts that brought you here initially, but it's sure to be the welcome, the hospitality, and the low-impact philosophy that'll keep you coming back.

## The Yurt Farm

Crynfryn, Penuwch, Tregaron, Ceredigion, SY25 6RE
www.theyurtfarm.co.uk

The 5 yurts are exceptionally well equipped with organic futons, bedding, all cooking equipment, including gas hob, a basket of farm goodies, a wood-burning stove plus logs, and kindling. There are even tea- and coffee-making facilities, charging points for phones and laptops, and a first-aid kit. Outside each yurt there's a BBQ or fire pit and a picnic table. The communal cabin has a well-equipped kitchen, wood-burning stove, and a comfy sofa as well as more cooking equipment, board games, a small library, and lots of extra bits and bobs such as toasty sandwich-makers to use on the fire. Next door is the compost loo and solar shower. There's also a sandpit, a swing, a woodshed yurt for extra firewood (which is free), and an 'honesty' farm shop with meat, veg, and jam for sale.

Details of a whole raft of days out can be found in the cabin, including Oakwood Theme Park (01834 891376; www.oakwoodthemepark.co.uk) and Dolaucothi Gold Mines (01558 650177) where you can try your hand at panning for gold; useful if you're planning an extravagant meal at the Harbourmaster Hotel (see p173).

Just over 3 miles away at Cross Inn is the traditional Rhos Yr Hafod Inn (01974 272644; www.rhos-yr-hafod-inn.co.uk) with the tiny windows, thick walls, crackling fires, and decorated oak beams that all old pubs should have. Foodies will want to head a bit further to Aberaeron harbour and the delightful Harbourmaster Hotel.

Open from April to October.

Weekly rates are £350 to £600, depending on the season and size of yurt; short breaks (£120 to £160) are also available.

cosy under canvas

Located in four acres of beautiful woodland and water meadow, in the heart of the Welsh/English borders countryside, sits Dolbedwyn House. Emma, the lady of Dolbedwyn, is warm and inviting, and, as she shows you around, you'll quickly see how one woman's touch can impress big time when it comes to your glamping experience.

Walking along the path through the woods, you can't fail to absorb all the feminine finesse oozing from the site. It is a woodland retreat like no other, a camping oxymoron: rugged, earthy daintiness; muddy, organised plots; rustic, frilly communal areas; and axes lying next to hammocks.

Tucking into a piece of Emma's home-made double-chocolate fudge cake and sipping a cup of tea, you won't know what to do next; run through the neighbouring fields laughing like a seven-year-old with a new toy, chop down some firewood like a true forester, or just laze in a hammock humming 'Zip-a-Dee-Doo-Dah' for a couple of hours. At some stage during your stay, Emma will also introduce you to the real lady of Dolbedwyn – Hattie the pig – who's as big as she is beautiful, and loved by kids of all ages.

Instead of the traditional tipi, Cosy Under Canvas' tipis are based on the Scandinavian Sami design. All tipis and the geodesic dome have been created using modern construction techniques and 21st-century materials to combat whatever the Welsh weather throws at them. But never mind the external details; the cosiness of Cosy Under Canvas can be found inside. Dazzling white, fluffy sheepskin rugs, a hand-carved chest of drawers filled with goodies, a wood-burning stove to warm your tootsies on, and a beautifully alluring bed.

Cosy Under Canvas is camping's equivalent of a steamy bubblebath; you will leave feeling as toasty and cosy as the inside of Emma's tipis.

## Cosy Under Canvas

Dolbedwyn, Newchurch, Kington, Powys, HR5 3QQ
www.cosyundercanvas.co.uk

🌿 Two raised tipis and 1 geodesic dome each sleep up to 4 people and contain a double futon bed and 2 roll-out futon mattresses. Inside, you'll find Welsh blankets, throws, a wooden storage box filled with tourist info, candles, a petrol lantern, and cotton bedding (for an additional charge). There's a chimenea on the decking and you can build a campfire in one of the designated pits, or if you prefer more conventional cooking there's a massive communal kitchen, BBQs, and tripod stands. Throw in games, compost loos, complimentary wood on arrival, recycling facilities, hammocks, wellie racks, fresh spring-water tanks, ice packs, and dry storage containers, and you're bound to be a very cosy and happy bunny.

🌿 The site lies in the Brecon Beacons National Park (01874 624437; www.breconbeacons.org), so any route you choose to take will be a walker's paradise. Nearby Hay-on-Wye is brilliant for rummaging around boutiques and galleries. Or, for something more active, canoe down the River Wye, 5 minutes from Hay's town centre (01497 847213; www.wyevalleycanoes.co.uk).

🌿 For a contemporary eatery, relax in the Globe (01497 821762; www.globeathay.org) with a Penguin Classic from one of Hay's bookshops. Voted one of the best dining pubs in Britain, the Three Tuns (01497 821855; www.three-tuns.com), also in Hay, is definitely a place to check out – and it does a cracking Sunday lunch to boot.

🌿 Open from late April to the end of October.

🌿 Tipis cost £195 to £550 per week, and the dome is £245 to £590 (depending on the season).

# eco retreats

## Eco Retreats

Plas Einion, Furnace, Machynlleth, Powys, SY20 8PG; www.ecoretreats.co.uk

🐾 Each of the 6 dwellings is set in its own idyllic location, where your only neighbour is the great outdoors. The tipis and yurts have everything you need, except food. A private eco-loo and spring mountain 'shower' are on the doorstep; solar-shower bags offer a warmer option.

🐾 Also included with an Eco Retreats break are tickets to the Centre for Alternative Technology (CAT, 01654 705950; www.cat.org.uk), Europe's leading eco-centre. It offers information and working displays on all things green. There's also the Museum of Modern Art (01654 703355) at Machynlleth; or tea shops in nearby Aberdyfi.

🐾 In Machynlleth head for the Wynnstay Hotel (01654 702941; www.wynnstay-hotel.com) – a gastropub with a great atmosphere (and good food) in the bar. And the fish and chips at Hennighans (01654 702761; www. hennighans.co.uk), also in Machynlleth, are hard to beat.

🐾 Open from April to November.

🐾 A weekend break for 2 is £339 for a tipi or £359 for a yurt. The price includes reiki, meditation, a small organic hamper, and a visit to CAT.

Run by reiki healers ChaNan and husband Michael, Eco Retreats is aimed at those campers who need to take a break from modern living. Five fully equipped tipis and a yurt are hidden away in a stunning, remote forest – as a place to chill, you won't find many options more horizontal than this.

The site's theme is peace and tranquillity, with a healthy dose of eco-living thrown in. To get you in the mood, the camping experience includes an individual session of reiki healing in the comfort of your own tipi or yurt and a soothing meditation as the sun sets. Even the most cynical of campers should give these experiences a whirl, as they transport your mind a zillion miles away from the stresses of life and work.

The drive into the retreat is an amazing experience in itself, as you negotiate dirt tracks through 600 acres of stunning pine forest and organic farmland. It's hard to believe that such remoteness exists in the UK. You may feel that you're never going to arrive, but keep following the hand-painted yellow signs and you'll end up in a leafy glade by a babbling brook surrounded by oak trees. This is probably the last time you'll bother to use your car until the sad day of your departure, when you'll be desperate to cling to the trees and declare your allegiance to all things green.

The dwellings are furnished in a relaxed, luxurious, and romantic way – from sheepskins strewn across the double bed to tea lights scattered on every surface. A pack of organic edible treats awaits you inside and all the necessary cooking paraphernalia is conveniently to hand. Heating is from both a wood-burning chimenea inside the tipi and an open fire outside. Either form of heat is particularly welcome when you run in from the cold spring-water shower – an unmissable, and totally exhilarating, experience.

Envelop yourself in the total Eco Retreats experience. Leave all your usual gizmos and gadgets at home. Just doze off listening to the fire crackling, and wake up to birdsong, running spring-water, and the wind in the trees. It's Zen and the art of camping.

# cledan valley
# tipis

It was love at first sight, owner Hywel Jones explained, recalling the moment he first laid eyes on a tipi. The image of one of these conical tents, tucked away in a woodland clearing, spurred Hywel to recreate the same enticing, hippyish vibe on this stunning spot in the heart of Wales' Cledan Valley. And, by Jones, has he done well.

Upon arrival you'll be greeted by Hywel's daughter, Beth, who will probably be chopping logs for the huge pile of communal firewood. 'It can take a couple of smoky days to get the hang of fire-building,' she laughs, as she hauls our bags on to her quad bike, 'but most get it right by the end.' She's not wrong: this site was made for campfire-lovers.

The eight tipis are scattered throughout an expanse of rolling meadow, and range in size from the snug Honeymoon tipi, rested on a secluded spot on the edge of the campsite, to the mammoth Red Kite – a huge 8.5-metre dwelling just begging for a roaring fire and a chorus of 'Kumbaya' at dusk.

Inside each tipi, you'll find retro futons, sheepskin rugs, and psychedelic mats, but the main attraction is unquestionably the large wood-burning fire pit. If the idea of making your own fire excites you, then prepare for some thrills while honing your fire-starter skills. The trick is to use dry wood with not too much bark. Build it big to keep the fire hot, and the smoke will be drawn upwards, keeping you cough-free, quietly smug, and snug.

The campsite has a healthy-looking carbon footprint too. The tipis are made down the road, in Llanbrynmair, and drinking water comes from the site's own natural spring.

The owners have stuck to their roots, and Cledan Valley tipis doesn't pretend to be anything it's not; the old-school vibe is genuine, heartfelt, and that's just how we (and the many regulars) like it.

## Cledan Valley Tipis

4 Bank House, Carno, Caersws, Powys, SY17 5LR
www.cledanvalleytipi.co.uk

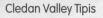 Despite its dangerous-sounding nature, fires are allowed inside all of the 8 tipis; some tipis also have a fire pit just outside. A small shower block houses a separate toilet and shower, plus there's a wash-room suitable for those with disabilities. There's a small children's play area, but most kids will be off discovering the hidden delights in 8 acres of meadow: hopping on to rope swings, building dens in the bracken, and exploring every nook and cranny.

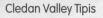 The Centre for Alternative Technology (01654 705950; www.cat.org.uk) in Machynlleth is a ready-made day out on all things eco. But don't leave without tramping about the local area on 2 feet. There are routes dotted around the Elan Valley for all levels of walker and cyclist. For adrenaline-fuelled action, spend an afternoon quad-biking at Ty Mawr (01654 702746). While retiring shoppers should head to the quaint market town of Llanidloes for its quirky boutiques.

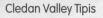 The Aleppo Merchant Inn (01686 420210; www.thealeppo.co.uk) is a favourite with locals and offers hearty pub grub and a decent pint. Further afield, Corris has lots of great pubs to choose from. For campsite cuisine, a hearty selection of local meats is stocked by the village Spar (01686 420550) – the Neuadd Fach sausages are tip-top. Pont Farm (01686 650896; www.pontfarmfoods. co.uk) can supply the greens, and their veg boxes can be ordered direct from the campsite.

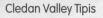 Open from Easter until the end of September.

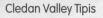 Tipis for 2–4 people are £350 to £400 per week and a 6–8-people tipi costs £500 to £775 per week.

strawberry
skys

In 2008 the British Household Panel Survey studied a random selection of British citizens to locate the happiest place in the land. The result? Powys, Wales. All that good, clean country living scored highly over cities, whose overcrowded streets and pack-em-in residential blocks were no contest for a county full of sheep and fields. When you meet the proprietor of Strawberry Skys [sic], Eric, the survey rings true; he comes across as someone who jumps into his wellies each morning eager to add the finishing touches to his new glamping paradise.

Eric and Anya decided to drop out of the rat race to buy a smallholding in the countryside. Cornwall was 'too full'; Scotland too far; Wales was just perfect. Having dreamed up the notion of running a mini yurt empire, they tested out a few established operations before getting to work. Eric admits he owes a lot of his inspiration to Larkhill Tipis (p140), where they stayed for a week. Winds were howling and rains bucketing down, but it didn't put the couple off and soon Strawberry Skys opened for business.

The site is a steep, narrow field facing hills in all directions. Sloping down to a valley floor, the only visible building is a hilltop farmhouse on the horizon. You've just the sheep for company and their job is to graze.

Eric's only bone of contention since moving to happy Powys is how fast the grass grows; the sheep help keep the blades short. Situated at the top, middle, and bottom of the slope are three Mongolian yurts (two that sleep two people and one sleeping four). Also at the foot of the hill is a fabulous all-mod-cons kitchen outbuilding with a veranda, compost loo, and hot-shower unit – all pretty, clean, and new.

Each yurt has been brightly painted in greens and oranges, while solar-powered fairy lights and natural coconut matting join rugs

and cushions from India. Wood-burners keep
guests toasty during winter months; Eric
brings wood around each evening. Fire pits
are flanked by chunky wooden tables and
benches, and each yurt has its own BBQ.
Sitting out all night chewing the fat and
chomping on hot dogs under paraffin lamps
doesn't get much more stylish than this.

Despite being just miles inland from the
English border, the site is burrowed deep
enough into Wales' bosom to hear the
country's provincial heartbeat. Yet because
it's within reach of motorways, escaping here
from most major cities is a breeze. In high
season, Eric runs bookings Friday to Monday
and Monday to Friday (or both) so there's no
excuse to avoid grabbing a long weekend after
a harrowing week at work. One of the site's
big appeals is that you can take it over entirely.
A few good books, some board games, and
hiking gear are all you need, whether there
are two of you, or a dozen. And bring some
good boots to tramp the unmarked footpath
that runs alongside the site, as even in the
summer there are soggy patches.

Convenient, cool, and waterproof,
Strawberry Skys' yurts are a big hit. Take
it from us; guests could not fail to leave
this camp feeling rested, revived, and, yes,
perfectly happy with life too.

## Strawberry Skys

Clyniarth Cottage, Cyfronydd, Welshpool, Powys, SY21 9HB; www.strawberryskys.co.uk

There are 3 yurts: 2 small yurts (sleep 2–4) and the larger yurt (sleeps 4–6). All firewood and kindling for the fire pits and wood-burners is free, as are the firelighters, matches, and tea lights. Eggs are sometimes available, free of charge. There are 2 compost loos (1 for each movement, as it were), a modern kitchen outbuilding, a shower block, and a pleasant terraced picnic area.

Whatever the weather, take a trip along the Welshpool & Llanfair Light Railway (01938 810441; www.wllr.org.uk) aboard one of the old-school carriages towed by a puffing steam locomotive from the early 1900s. It makes a stylish and romantic way of taking in all the gorgeous Powys scenery. Or you can explore the countryside on foot, straight from the site. And there are always the shops in nearby Welshpool or Newtown to browse if you have had too much fresh air.

There are 3 pubs within walking distance (1½ miles away in Llanfair Caereinion): the Black Lion, the Goat, and the Red Lion. Pop into Welshpool for some Welsh Black beef for your campfire from the excellent butcher Rikki Lloyd (01983 552683; www.rikkilloyd.co.uk). Or sample the excellent Sunday lunches at the 17th-century oak-beamed Lion Hotel & Restaurant (01686 640452; www.thelionhotelberriew.com), 4 miles away in Berriew.

Open from February to November.

Prices range from £150 for a 2-night (minimum) stay in a small yurt during low season to £400 for a 3-night weekend/4-night midweek break in the large yurt in high season. Exclusive use for up to 10 adults (or a group of 14 adults and children mix) will set you back £600 for 2 nights in low season or £1,000 in high season (a strict-no-noise-after-midnight policy exists here).

broome
retreat

After a few wrong turns and some unexpected off-roading, Broome Retreat finally came into view at the top of a narrow track in the quaint little village of Pen-y-Garnedd. Any woes were quickly forgotten, as there's a genuine, homely feel to this campsite from the off.

The two well-dressed yurts sit neatly at either end of a gently sloping field at the back of the owners' cottage. Being so close means Pete and Kate are on hand for anything you need. And once you're settled in, you're free to unwind and soak up the naturally laid-back vibe that oozes from every corner.

And what a place to unwind. With just one person to every 10 acres, Powys is one of the most sparsely populated districts in the land. Broome Retreat is tucked away in a remote corner of the beautiful Tanat Valley. If you're after breathtaking views and a healthy dose of tranquillity, then this is the landscape jackpot.

On site, the facilities have a certain rustic charm about them, including a toilet that is a serious contender for 'best view from a loo'. Next door, the stable has been converted into a homely kitchen, complete with wood-burning stove and rainy-day entertainment.

Inside, the yurts are delightfully presented and wonderfully cosy. As evening falls, the interior comes alive with the soft glow of fairy lights, plus enough tea lights dotted around to give IKEA a run for its money. Outside, the faint sparkle of solar lights and steadily burning campfires bring a casual sense of serenity. Simply settle down with a glass of vino, marvel over the clarity of the night sky, and enjoy the old-school charm of camping, but without a roll-mat in sight.

Whether you want to get in touch with your creative side, pull on your walking boots and head for the hills, or simply escape the hustle and bustle, come and revel in this sizeable slice of camping perfection.

## Broome Retreat

Tyn-y-Pant, Pen-y-Garnedd, Llanrhaeadr-ym-
Mochnant, Powys, SY10 0AN
www.broomeretreat.co.uk

🔥 Campfires are positively encouraged at these
2 cosy yurts. The rustic outhouse provides one flush
toilet and a powerful shower. Books and games
are provided in the kitchen, but the main attraction
is the plentiful outdoor space. Equally perfect for
a group (you can book out the whole site for
uninterrupted R&R), as well as couples seeking
a romantic weekend away, Broome Retreat is so
laid-back and flexible that you can mould a trip
here into your ideal excursion.

🔥 To go with the calm and cool vibe, ask Kate
to book you in for a session of massage, reiki,
aromatherapy, or acupuncture. In stark contrast,
Lake Bala is a must for water-loving adrenaline
junkies. Elsewhere, marvel at Pistyll Rhaeadr (at
75 metres, it's the tallest single-drop waterfall in the
UK), or simply go hill-walking around Snowdonia.
On rainy days, kids can get their hands dirty at Park
Hall Farm (01691 671123; www.parkhallfarm.co.uk)
just over the border in Oswestry.

🔥 In Llanfyllin, Seeds (01691 648604) is a relaxed
(albeit pricey) little bistro, serving modern British
food alongside a great wine list. For an abundance
of local produce, head to Down to Earth (01691
648841), a delightful small co-operative.

🔥 Open from April to the end of October.

🔥 A week in a yurt (sleeping 4) costs £360; short
breaks are £35 per adult per night.

anglesey tipis
and yurts

*Mam Cymru.* The Mother of Wales. Whatever you call it, Anglesey – separated from the mainland only by the narrow Menai Strait – exudes Welsh heritage. Its rich history has been passed down from its Celtic, Viking, and medieval settlers, and its people remain a predominantly Welsh-speaking population; so much so that you can almost feel the earth pulsating in time to their national anthem – '*Hen Wlad Fy Nhadau*'.

Anglesey isn't overrun with luxury camping options. But head to the east side of the island, just outside Brynteg, and you'll soon find that the hidden oasis of Anglesey Tipi and Yurt Holidays has got the glamping side of things well and truly covered.

Refreshingly, owners Charlie and Ela know that creating a great glampsite takes more than just plonking a few yurts and tipis in a field and watching the cash roll in. This campsite is clearly a labour of love, a way of life, and their *raison d'être*. This is a constantly evolving, living, breathing campsite, and they work year-round to ensure that this peaceful haven keeps getting better and better.

The site itself is well thought-out and a delight to visit – the clearings are carved out of the wilderness to create five tranquil spaces. Charlie and Ela are attentive hosts, and consideration for their campers is evident throughout; there are wheelbarrows on hand to transport your weekend bags (consider this when you're at home packing), and delicious home-grown veg is available to buy on site. Ela's recently honed weaving skills have been put to good use in creating a winding tunnel for kids to run through, and there's a patch of woodland left just wild enough for you to feel like you're the first person to discover it.

There are two tipis and three yurts dotted around the main camping space. Inside each, you'll find plenty of cooking implements, plus

enough fluffy cushions and sheepskin rugs to make your dwelling delightfully welcoming. Each yurt has a wood-burning stove, and each tipi has a small BBQ, plus there's a communal fire pit and sheltered area where campers gather come the twilight hours. They get extra brownie points for their eco credentials too. Recycling? Check. Compost loo? Check.

Anglesey Tipi and Yurt Holidays is the camping equivalent to chicken noodle soup; it's a great pick-me-up, and you feel a whole lot better after trying it. This is sustainable camping for peace-seeking visitors, and the best way to discover what makes it so magical is to come and see it for yourself.

The site might be a fair way out of town, but that just adds to its charming nature. Once you've snuggled into a woodland hammock, leaving the site will be the last thing on your mind. But if you can tear yourself away, take to the Isle of Anglesey Coastal Path for some truly breathtaking walks and views; you'll find sweeping sandy beaches and towering cliffs. While you're at it, why not try your hand at kayaking, coasteering, gorge-scrambling, or sea level traversing — exhilarating scrambling along cliffs, just above the breaking waves — with the guys from Anglesey Adventures? Spend a week here and you might just discover your new *raison d'être*.

## Anglesey Tipi and Yurt Holidays

Cae'r Gseg, Brynteg, Anglesey, LL78 8JT
www.angleseytipis.co.uk

There are 2 tipis (sleeping 2 or 4) and 3 yurts (sleeping 4 or 5); plus 2 flush toilets and 1 compost loo. There are 2 powerful showers (wash-rooms are to be refurbished for 2011). Campfires are allowed in designated areas. Kids of all sizes can play away in the wild woodland area, and there are hammocks for the grown-ups to relax in.

Follow the Isle of Anglesey Coastal Path to explore the stunning coastline, or hop on to a Puffin Island cruise (01248 810251; www.starida.co.uk) for a different perspective. Budding lepidopterists will enjoy the moths and butterflies at Pili Palas nature world (01248 712474; www.pilipalas.co.uk), while thrill-seekers can scale new heights at the Beacon Climbing Centre (08454 508222; www.beaconclimbing.com), near Llanberis.

The Menai Bridge is a fantastic hub for foodies; there are heaps of great local producers around, plus a monthly farmers' market. Relax in Grade II-listed style at the Bull Hotel (01248 722119; www.bullhotelanglesey.co.uk), which serves well-priced hearty mains.

Open from April to the end of November (September for the 2 tipis and 4-person yurt).

Prices are per night and get cheaper the longer you stay: a 2-person tipi costs £50 to £60; 4-person tipi £60 to £80; 4-person yurt £70 to £96; the Mongolian yurts cost £88 to £120.

# roulotte retreat

In the 19th century Sir Walter Scott, yeoman, novelist, and romantic balladeer, almost single-handedly created the kitsch Scottish heritage industry of tartan, tinned shortbread, clan chiefs, and bagpipes. Tasked with what would now be called 'branding' the visit of the newly crowned George IV to his northern kingdom, Scott turned tartan into the denim of its day, even decking the new king out in a fetching kilt. Of course, nowadays people are probably more familiar with the Scotland of *Trainspotting* than the romanticised world of Scott's novels but, still, old Walt has a lot to answer for.

His impressive baronial pile – Abbotsford – is nearby, but if you're looking for somewhere to stay that's not quite so grand here's an idea: a home that's designed to travel with you. After all, who can fail to feel the lure of life on the open road? With an old nag called Patience to tow your gypsy caravan along quiet country lanes, you can stop where you fancy, light a little fire, and cook your evening meal before lighting your pipe, and watching the stars spin until it's time for bed. Well, it's a nice idea at least, and so much better than battling home on the Northern Line or commuting on the A34.

Fans of *Cool Camping: France* will be familiar with the concept of the gypsy roulotte, the ornate wooden caravans of the Roma, which are a feature of Gallic glamping. And anyone who's ever visited Les Roulottes de la Serve in Beaujolais country may even be able to recognise the handiwork of its very own Pascal Patin here at Roulotte Retreat, by the Eildon Hills in the Scottish Borders.

Pascal's built a couple of the caravans here too, so in this appealing little site in a perfect meadow with a tumbling stream and a

scattering of roulottes, you can go some way to realising your freewheeling dream. All that's missing is dear old Patience. And the open road, of course.

Site-owners Alan and Avril have gone to huge lengths to source the roulottes and have them built and brought over from the continent. They're hand-crafted in beautiful wood and ornately furnished, with sumptuous fabrics. Each caravan has its own very distinctive feel. One, for example, is Indian-themed, with carved peacocks combined with paisley patterns. Another is a kind of Celtic–Moroccan affair. Inside, the fixtures, fittings, and soft furnishings are an eclectic mix of bespoke pieces, items picked up from Alan and Avril's travels around the world, and stuff from Scottish antique shops.

It all makes for an enchanting brew. Add in a solid Scottish mill house, a river, and a ruined mill nearby, a lochan to dip your feet (or your body) into, and amiable owners, and you have a recipe for a cracking place to hang out.

If you fancy saluting the sun then join Avril, who teaches yoga, for a session; there's a small studio available for all sorts of activities. Beyond the site there's a whole expanse of hilly countryside at your beck and call. Or, of course, you could just cosy up in your roulotte and read some of Sir Walter Scott's finest.

### Roulotte Retreat

Bowden, Melrose, Scottish Borders, TD6
www.roulotteretreat.com

🐾 A scattering of roulottes across a lovely meadow. All facilities are en suite to each roulotte, so there's a shower and separate toilet (with home-made soaps), a cooker, and wood-burning stove, plus independent heating. Towels and linen are included too. The water feature in the meadow, though smallish, is deep enough for a dip, and Avril offers yoga lessons, either one-to-one or in a group.

🐾 There's so much to do in the Borders it's difficult to know where to start. How about some fishing, horse-riding, birdwatching, or walking? The St Cuthbert's Way, which goes to from Melrose to Lindisfarne, runs right by the site. Most of the local towns have what are known as Common Ridings, ancient traditions involving hundreds of riders, usually held in June. How about a trip into Melrose, with its famous ruined abbey, equally famous Rugby Sevens (held in April), or its growing Book Festival (held in June)?

🐾 Home-baked bread can be ordered in advance (along with milk and newspapers), and a fish van comes by the site on various days of the week. There's also a veggie van on Thursdays and Fridays. Or Avril can organise a hamper of local produce for you with the cost based on what you want to include. For treats, head into Melrose, where either Marmions Brasserie (01896 822245) or the Townhouse (01896 822645) will offer you local fare, such as cullen skink, smoked venison, seared pigeon, and the like.

🐾 Open all year; however, access can be tricky in the snowy season.

🐾 Prices range from between £90 and £95 per night in low season to between £115 and £135 per night in high season, and depend on the roulotte.

lochhouses

Lochhouses Farm used to be the only Scottish outpost of the Feather Down Farms empire, the chain of sites for pampered campers who like their creature comforts; the chain about which everyone has an opinion. Like Marmite or Mandelson, you either love 'em or hate 'em, but there's no denying their success.

The Dale family who own the Lochhouses site took the decision to strike out on their own with a similar concept. You still get all the feathery and downy creature comforts you'd expect – fresh linen, clean towels, enough culinary gadgets to keep celebrity chefs amused for hours – but without any corporate booking forms and extra charges for this and that. And, instead of the dark brown tents of Feather Down, Lochhouses now has seven similar-sized safari-style tents in creamy beige. They're essentially the same thing: all-canvas with a comfy interior and wood-burning stove, but the new safari tents boast a covered porch.

The huge camping field at Lochhouses is a mile or so down a track from the Dales' farmhouse, which is itself a good mile or so from a minor road; it sits just behind a sizeable dune shielding it from sea winds. So, the only invading noises are from the wind whispering in the pine trees, hens clucking, and ponies munching grass in the field next door.

The safari tents are neatly placed around the periphery of the site, leaving plenty of privacy for campers and space in which to roam. By the entrance there's an old beached lobster-catcher boat that serves as a small tuck shop, with basic provisions inside if you run short; it's a long way back to civilisation from here.

Once you've settled in and fed the hens, clamber up the dunes to take in the views of the coast, from Bass Rock in the north down to the ruined castle of Dunbar on the promontory to the south. Dead ahead is an

expanse of the North Sea with just the odd passing cruise ship out on the horizon.

The south-east coast of Scotland must be the least visited part of a country that's always crawling with tourists. With the aortic artery of the A1 slicing through the land, perhaps it's no surprise that most folk coming from the south, from the Romans to the English armies, have made a beeline for Edinburgh without stopping – unless, of course, there was a Scottish army standing in their way.

But there's a host of reasons to explore this stretch of coast. There are cliffs, castles, sandy bays, and battlefields, as well as a Domesday directory of ancient villages. And nowadays there's the John Muir Country Park. Not as well known, even in Scotland, as he deserves to be, John Muir was a pioneer wilderness conservationist born in Dunbar in the 1830s. He emigrated to the US and played a huge part in the establishment of national parks there, including the gem at Yosemite. His memorial park in East Lothian is on a slightly smaller scale but still stretches along several miles of the coast from the ruined castle at Dunbar, along Belhaven Bay (past the campsite), and on towards Bass Rock.

And Lochhouses Farm is a handy 45-minute drive from Edinburgh, which is probably where you were heading in the first place.

## Lochhouses Farm

Tyninghame, nr Dunbar, East Lothian, EH42 1XP
www.harvestmoonholidays.com

There are 6 safari tents (sleeping up to 8) and a deluxe honeymoon tent (sleeps up to 6). Each tent has a wood-burning stove and oven, sink, flushing toilet, and hot shower. What was the old shower block has been remodelled into a kids' play area, and a beached lobster boat has a tuck shop inside for all the basics. To cut down on your packing, you can add a towel package for £5 per person per stay but linen is included. And if you fancy cooking on an open-air fire, hire a special pot to rustle up a warming stew on chillier days (£10 per night).

Explore on feet, horseback, or cycle the myriad paths and trails through the John Muir Country Park; there's pony hire at the farm next door and bikes of all sizes can be rented on site. A 15-minute drive will take you to see Concorde at the National Museum of Flight (03001 236789; see www.nms.ac.uk).

For a local pub, head to East Linton. The typical red-brick Crown Hotel (01620 860335) has a good range of ales and whiskies despite being a little 'Laura Ashley', while the Linton Hotel (01620 860202) is similarly smart. Both serve cracking meals.

Open all year.

Prices per safari tent are £475 to £875 for a week, £350 to £550 for a weekend, or £345 to £525 for a midweek break (depending on the season).

comrie croft

Comrie Croft is the very model of a modish modern campsite – it's environmentally friendly, it combines secluded woodland pitches with two camping meadows for family tents, it allows campfires and has a communal fire pit complete with shelter from a massive military cargo-chute, which you can all sit around and get to know your neighbours.

Five kåtas are dotted among the woodland; an easy access kåta sits in the lower camping meadow. These Swedish tipi-style tents are set on wooden decking and are large enough to house a family of six. They come with sheepskin rugs, hand-crafted furniture, and a bunch of logs for the wood-burning stove. Up here in the woods you are hidden by trees and bracken, so you can feel like you have the place to yourself, but the price of all that woodland tranquillity is that vehicles have to be left at reception. Best, then, to come for a week to make it worthwhile humping all your gear through the forest. Mind you, it's a small price to pay to camp in such glorious surroundings.

A little pond above the wood is fed by a stream at one end, which spills out from the other side of the pond and burbles down through the trees. In the evening the sound of the water vies with the crackle of campfires and roasting sausages, while the smoke helps keep any winged monsters at bay.

The nearby town of Crieff is something of a one-street tourist affair, and if you fancy reacquainting yourself with 'town living' you're better off going the extra mile to Perth, a delightful product of the Georgian enthusiasm for the neoclassical. It's all far grander than a wee town on the banks of the Tay deserves, but then that's its unique appeal. It also has quite some history behind it, being a former capital of Scotland and close to Scone Palace, the coronation site of ancient Scottish kings. There's a replica here of the Stone of Destiny,

the coronation stone on which new monarchs
would sit to be crowned. The original was
'borrowed' by Edward I, taken to Westminster,
and has been used to crown English and British
kings ever since. It was stolen back in the 1950s
by some enterprising Scottish students, and,
although it was recovered and returned to
Westminster, rumours have always persisted
that the stone they handed back was a replica
and that the real one is still secreted away
somewhere in Scotland. So when, after Scottish
Devolution, the Westminster Stone of Destiny
was returned to Scotland permanently, no one
knew if it was the real deal or not.

There's no doubting the authenticity of
Comrie Croft, though. This is how modern
camping should be and it makes an ideal
introduction to canvas adventures. It's also a
painless way of easing yourself into Scotland.
This part of Perthshire's pretty well-heeled, a
land of gentleman farmers and classy spas, and
a far cry from the more rugged landscapes as
you head north up the A9 past Pitlochry. But
then not everyone wants the full-on lochs and
heather experience. At least not at first. Cut
your teeth on the sloping fields and woods of
central Perthshire. Or perhaps you'll find that
Comrie Croft's just the kind of thing you've
been looking for and decide you don't need
to take another step. And who can blame you?

## Comrie Croft

Braincroft, Crieff, Perthshire, PH7 4JZ
www.comriecroft.com

The 5 kåta tents (sleeping 4 adults or a family of 6) are built on wooden platforms, with their own wood-burning stoves to keep you toasty whatever the weather. Each has everything you need, from sheepkins and comfy cushions to camp cooking essentials, and a huge sack of wood to start you off (more available at £5 per sack). Outside, each kåta has a hammock, a brazier for a campfire, and an outdoor shelter. You share the spotlessly fresh facilities with the other tent campers: a shower/toilet block, and outside recycling and dishwashing facilities. Next to the woods is a compost toilet so no treks to answer a call of nature. There's a shop at reception (with more loos) where you can buy firewood, milk, free-range eggs, local butcher's sausages, and other basics. There's also a fresh drinking-water tap and a 24-hour tea and coffee machine. Mountain bikes are available to hire too.

Onsite there's an orienteering course and kids' treasure hunt. Further afield, make the trip to Scone Palace (01738 552300; www.scone-palace.net), just north of Perth. It's the original home of the contentious Stone of Destiny. There's a replica here now, the real one being in Edinburgh. Or so they'd have you believe.

Eat at the Royal (01764 679200) in Comrie. Part of the Royal Hotel, it's towards the end of the main street in a square on the right. Choose between the hotel's posh bar or the more pubby affair at the side.

Open all year.

Prices for a kåta are £168 to £308 for a week, £88 to £144 for a weekend, or £100 to £200 for a midweek break (depending on the season).

the
shielings

The Isle of Mull, despite being one of the most southerly and easiest to access of the Inner Hebridean islands, is surprisingly unspoilt and very little molested by the tourist industry. Just about all the visitors to the island arrive on the impressive Caledonian MacBrayne ship, the *MV Isle of Mull*, which sails from Oban to the island's ferry terminal at Craignure. That such numbers travel to and from this sleepy little bay is quite bizarre. The two-hourly drama can be watched from The Shielings campsite: for a few minutes the place is thick with folk, then when the ship disappears, the place is deserted once again, and you wonder if it was all just a dream.

The Shielings stands on the edge of the bay, overlooking not only the ferry terminal but also a colossal vista of glorious West Highland scenery, taking in the Sound of Mull and Loch Linnhe, beyond which stand the highest mountains in Britain. Besides having an extraordinary view, The Shielings campsite offers a variety of fixed 'shielings', which can be hired by the night or by the week.

These shielings are all-weather tents that come equipped with beds, tables, chairs, a kitchen, and a heater; the posher models also have en suite bathrooms. Those without an en suite can use the site's excellent facilities, so there's no need to rough it here.

Should you eventually tire of the view and the comings and goings at the ferry terminal, you can't help but notice, or indeed hear, the Isle of Mull Steam Railway chuntering back and forth along the seaward edge of the site. The station is just 100 metres away, and from there a narrow-gauge train takes passengers just over a mile to Torosay Castle and Gardens. In early summer the gardens are bright enough to hurt sensitive southern eyes, so remember to pack your shades. Another couple of scenic away-from-it-all miles on foot towards Duart

Point reveal one of Scotland's classic sights, Duart Castle, which grows gradually more imposing as you approach. Back to Craignure, and if you've brought along a canoe or two, or even a boat, these can be launched at the front of the site where there's a handy slip road straight into the Sound of Mull.

From Mull you can get to the mainland quickly using the Fishnish–Lochaline ferry five miles north of the Shielings; it can seem easier to reach than other places that are actually on the mainland, such as Morvern or Ardnamurchan, which are incredibly remote.

Bring your bikes to Mull for some serious traffic-free miles and a wilderness experience unlike anywhere else in Britain. There's an excellent cycle ride to the island's main (and only) town at Tobermory, at the northern end of Mull. It's a 40-mile round trip, but taken over the whole day, and in decent weather, it isn't nearly as arduous as it is scenic.

The island has always been famous for its wildlife, and especially its population of sea eagles. They can usually be seen around Loch Frisa, where there are organised eagle-spotting trips, but also at several other coastal areas on the island. Thankfully, you don't need to be eagle-eyed to appreciate the spectacular beauty of this island, and the Shielings is the perfect base from which to explore it all.

## The Shielings

Craignure, Isle of Mull, PA65 6AY
www.shielingholidays.co.uk

🦆 You can choose from 8 en suite sheilings (1 of which has a bath) or there are 7 other ones without. The site has excellent amenities, including free hot showers, toilets, washbasins, disabled facilities, and a family bathroom with bath. There's also a shieling common room with multi-fuel stove, a games shieling, and a laundrette. Learn about the abundant wildlife in this haven (www.shielingwildlife.co.uk). 'Checklists' are provided free of charge, so children can head out creature-spotting around the site and shoreline, ticking off the various species of shell, flora, and abundant wildlife they find. CDs and albums documenting the birds, red deer, sea otters, dolphins, and porpoises that visit the site are also available at reception, giving details on the best times to see them, along with a map telling you where.

🦆 There are only a couple of pubs in the area and, thankfully, they're good ones. The Craignure Inn (01680 812305; www.craignure-inn.co.uk), a mere 200 metres away, has a varied menu and also does takeaway pizzas. MacGregor's Roadhouse (01680 812471) is also handy, with top-notch grub.

🦆 Torosay Castle and Gardens (01680 812421; www.torosay.com) are a 10-minute walk from the site. The Scottish Sealife Sanctuary (01631 720386; www.sealsanctuary.co.uk) is about 10 miles away in Barcaldine and has an impressive array of water-loving creatures, including sharks. The Isle of Mull Hotel (08709 506267) has a lovely swimming pool and spa facilities if you fancy a spot of 'me' time.

🦆 Open from early April to mid October.

🦆 En suite shielings are £45 per night for 2 people and a week is £290; shielings without a bathroom cost £30 per night for 2 people or £195 per week.

**Acknowledgements**

*Glamping Getaways*

Series Concept and Series Editor: Jonathan Knight
Researched and written by: Shelley Bowdler,
Sophie Dawson, Keith Didcock, Jonathan Knight,
Paul Marsden, Andrea Oates, Sam Pow, Amy Sheldrake,
Susan Smith, Andy Stothert, Clover Stroud, Paul Sullivan,
Alexandra Tilley Loughrey, Richard Waters, Dixe Wills,
and Harriet Yeomans

Managing Editor: Sophie Dawson
Editor: Nikki Sims
Designer: Nicola Erdpresser
Cover Design: Nicola Erdpresser
Proofreader: Leanne Bryan
Editorial Assistant: Harriet Yeomans
Marketing: Shelley Bowdler

Published by: Punk Publishing, 3 The Yard, Pegasus Place,
London, SE11 5SD

Distributed by: Portfolio Books, 2nd Floor, Westminster
House, Kew Road, Richmond, Surrey, TW9 2ND

All photographs © Shelley Bowdler, Sophie Dawson,
Keith Didcock, Jonathan Knight, Paul Marsden, Andrea
Oates, Sam Pow, Amy Sheldrake, Susan Smith, Andy
Stothert, Clover Stroud, Paul Sullivan, Alexandra Tilley
Loughrey, Richard Waters, Dixe Wills, and Harriet
Yeomans, except the following (all reproduced with
permission): pp22, 23, 25 © Apex Pictures/Chris Saville;
p24 © Cornish Tipi Holidays; pp26–27 © Belle Tents;
p77 © Shadow Woods; p106 © Sarah Legge Photography;
pp120–125 © Long Valley Yurts; pp126–129 © Full
Circle; p131 © Pot-a-Doodle Do; p147 © Annwn Valley
Yurts; pp8, 170–174 © Under the Thatch/Greg
Stevenson; p189 © Strawberry Skys; p204 © Roulotte
Retreat; p211 © Lochhouses/Monica Loudon;
p218 © The Shielings/Andy Kirkham.

Front cover photograph © Marcus Lyon
(www.theglassworks.co.uk)
Additional retouching by Paul Cochrane

The publishers and authors have done their best to ensure
the accuracy of all information in *Glamping Getaways*,
however, they can accept no responsibility for any injury,
loss or inconvenience sustained by anyone as a result of
information contained in this book.

Punk Publishing takes its environmental responsibilities
seriously. This book has been printed on paper made from
renewable sources and we continue to work with our
printers to reduce our overall environmental impact.
Wherever possible, we recycle, eat organic food, and
always turn the tap off when brushing our teeth.

## HAPPY CAMPERS?

We hope you've enjoyed reading
*Glamping Getaways* and that it's inspired
you to get out there. The campsites featured
in this book are a personal selection chosen
by the Cool Camping team. We have visited
hundreds of campsites across the UK to find
this selection, and we hope you like them as
much as we do. However, it hasn't been possible
to visit every single UK glampsite. So, if you
know of a special place that you think should
be included, we'd like to hear about it. Send an
email telling us the name and location of the
site, some contact details and why it's special.
We'll credit all useful contributions in the next
edition of the book, and senders of the best
emails will receive a complimentary copy.
Thanks and see you out there!
enquiries@punkpublishing.co.uk